LILLIAN HELLMAN

Lillian Hellman

An Imperious Life

DOROTHY GALLAGHER

Yale

UNIVERSITY

PRESS

New Haven and London

Yale University Press books may be purchased in quantity for educational,
business, or promotional use. For information, please e-mail sales.press@yale.edu
(U.S. office) or sales@yaleup.co.uk (U.K. office).

Set in Janson type by Integrated Publishing Solutions, Grand Rapids, Michigan.
Printed in the United States of America.

Library of Congress Cataloging-in-Publication Data
Gallagher, Dorothy.
Lillian Hellman : an imperious life / Dorothy Gallagher.
pages cm. — (Jewish Lives)
Includes bibliographical references and index.
ISBN 978-0-300-16497-8 (cloth : alk. paper)
1. Hellman, Lillian, 1905–1984—Criticism and interpretation.   2. Dramatists,
American—20th century—Biography.   3. Women dramatists, American—
Biography.   I. Title.
PS3515.E343Z686 2013
812'.52—dc23
[B]
2013027579

A catalogue record for this book is available from the British Library.

This paper meets the requirements of ANSI/NISO Z39.48–1992
(Permanence of Paper).

10 9 8 7 6 5 4 3 2 1

Frontispiece: Author Lillian Hellman smoking a cigarette as she chats with author
Dashiell Hammett while dining at Club 21. (Photo by George Karger/Pix Inc./
Time Life Pictures/Getty Images)

CONTENTS

CONTENTS

Prologue

AT THE height of her celebrity—and it is difficult to say exactly when that would have been, since she was almost un-flaggingly famous over a period of five decades—Lillian Hell-man was as glamorous and visible a public presence as any movie star. But let's say that one peak moment came in 1939, with the opening of *The Little Foxes*, which was her second hit play. Hellman was thirty-four years old. The play opened in February, which would have given her the opportunity to wear the furs she loved, a new mink in this case. She was seldom in public without her friends, and she would have been seen with Dashiell Hammett, her tall, handsome lover; and with her di-rector and soon-to-be lover, Herman Shumlin; with her friend Dorothy Parker; and perhaps with the very glamorous Sara and Gerald Murphy, whom she had met in Paris. When Hellman appeared at restaurants, theater openings, and at the best par-ties, she was beautifully coiffed and made up. When reporters wanted to interview her in 1939, they came to her suite at the Plaza Hotel.

From 1934, when her first play, *The Children's Hour*, had been a Broadway hit, through the early 1960s, Hellman produced a play almost every other year. Between plays she wrote screenplays. If not every one of her plays was a hit, still, for thirty years, Hellman was the queen of Broadway playwrights. In fact, she was the only woman playwright of her generation. In those years, when people spoke of the American theater, they spoke of Eugene O'Neill, Clifford Odets, and Hellman; a few years later they would add the names of Arthur Miller, Tennessee Williams, and William Inge.

Much later, sometime in the late 1960s, or early seventies, I stepped onto a crowded elevator and caught my first and only glimpse of Lillian Hellman. She was unmistakable, though smaller than I would have thought. (A "mighty little woman," Norman Mailer once said of her; an admiring phrase, even when placed in his complete sentence: "Oh, she was mean, manipulative and heroic—she was a mighty little woman."[1])

By the time I saw her in the elevator, Hellman was in her mid-sixties; her plays had all been written, and the first of her three volumes of memoirs, *An Unfinished Woman*, had recently been published. If I hadn't yet read the book, I did soon after that elevator sighting, and I then passed on the book to my mother, who was, as I knew, a fan of Hellman's. My mother admired Hellman's plays, particularly her anti-Fascist play *Watch on the Rhine*; she admired Hellman even more for her outspoken political views, which, like her own, often echoed the views of the Communist Party; she admired Hellman almost as much for having lived openly with a man to whom she was not married. And, of course, my mother admired her, as so many did, for Hellman's courageous testimony before the House Committee on Un-American Activities.

Hellman was Jewish, as my family was, a fact she did not make much of, nor did we, but which was nevertheless central to our sense of ourselves in the world. Apart from the fact that Hellman was rich and famous, and we did not know any rich and famous people, Hellman seemed exactly like the sort of person we would know—bohemian (although Park Avenue in her personal style), opinionated, and politically one of us. This is by way of saying that I do not come to Lillian Hellman tabula rasa.

Lillian Hellman died in 1984. Four full-scale biographies have since been devoted to her life and work. The first was begun while she was still alive, the last appeared less than two years ago. There is also a fifth book that is a double biography of Hellman and Dashiell Hammett and their near-marriage of thirty years. There are a number of biographies of Hammett that naturally include material about Hellman, and a collection of Hammett's letters, many of which are written to Hellman. Still another book about Hellman is an apparently affectionate reminiscence of a long friendship, but it is ultimately a devastating portrait of a desperate woman in her declining years.

These are a lot of books even for a mighty little woman. The numbers indicate that even thirty years after her death Hellman excites interest. Not only as a writer, which would be reason enough, but as a conundrum—a woman whose determination to prevail in all aspects of her life was often at odds with the persona of moral rectitude she presented to the world. "The power of LH—a puzzlement," Elizabeth Hardwick wrote to Mary McCarthy, "even when one knows how concentrated she has been in its service."[2] Everyone who has written about Hellman runs smack into her capacity to outrage, and to enrage. Hellman was a woman of enormous energy—talented, ambitious, restless, audacious, highly sexual, funny, generous, avaricious, mendacious, demanding, greedy, contemptuous, dogmatic, irritable, mean, jealous, self-righteous, angry. To use an ambiguous phrase, Lillian Hellman was a piece of work.

Lillian Hellman was born in New Orleans in 1905. Her mother was Julia Newhouse, of Demopolis, Alabama; her father was Max Hellman, born in New Orleans. The couple married in 1904, and for the first six years of their daughter's life, the Hellmans lived with Max Hellman's sisters, Jenny and Hannah, who ran a boarding house on Prytania Street, at the edge of New Orleans' famous Garden District.

Julia brought a sizeable dowry to the marriage, which her husband used to open a shoe manufacturing company. The business failed. In 1910 or 1911, the Hellmans followed Julia's family to New York, where Max Hellman got a job as a traveling salesman. Lillian attended public school in New York for most of the school year; for the remaining months she went back to New Orleans to live with her aunts. She graduated from high school in New York in 1922, went to New York University for two years, then made her entrance into the literary world with a job at Boni and Liveright, then the foremost publishing house in New York.

In 1925, Hellman married Arthur Kober, a theatrical press agent and writer. They soon moved to Hollywood where Kober wrote screenplays and Hellman got a job reading scripts for a movie company. Five years after her marriage, Hellman met Dashiell Hammett. She divorced Kober, and she and Hammett remained more or less together, in a complicated arrangement, for the rest of Hammett's life. In 1934, with Hammett providing the source material, and editorial expertise, Hellman wrote her first play, *The Children's Hour.* It was a hit. She was twenty-nine. A long career and an unimaginably eventful life lay ahead.

Hellman was an only child, and as far as the record shows, a well-loved child. Her father seems to have been a feckless and humorous man, her mother abstracted and fey. Her paternal aunts, who were unmarried women of strong character, loomed large in her early life. Many only children grow up with a strong sense of entitlement, and Hellman certainly had that. By her own testimony she was headstrong and willful from a very early age. She was never pretty, and there is no doubt that all her life she suffered from her lack of beauty, although it never seemed to impede her very active sexual life. Money was a central ingredient in the lives of her mother's family; they had a lot of it, originating in the fortune made by Hellman's great-grandfather, Isaac Marx, who began his career as a peddler in antebellum Alabama. By comparison, the Hellmans were poor relations, and money was a preoccupation of Hellman's work, and of her life, too.

Hellman lived much of her life in public, which should make her a congenial subject for a biographer. But the opposite is true. She did not want her biography written, and while she was alive she destroyed letters and personal papers, and insisted that her friends refuse to speak to inquiring strangers. She wanted her memoirs to stand for her life. But, as it turned out, much of what Hellman claimed to remember could not be relied on for its actual truth. Like a mirror image of Hansel and Gretel, she often strewed her breadcrumbs so as *not* to lead home.

Since there are biographies of Hellman that follow a chronological path, I have given most attention to the aspects of her life that particularly interested me. I was interested in the story of Isaac Marx, Hellman's great-grandfather, who emigrated from Europe to rural, antebellum Alabama. I wondered how these immigrants were received when they first appeared in the agricultural South in the 1840s. What kind of lives did they make in a place where they were exotics, without language or farming skills? How did they manage to thrive economically, as so many of them did? What sort of relations did they have with slaves, and slave owners? How did they fare in the Civil War and Reconstruction? And what did Hellman, a third-generation descendant of the immigrant Isaac Marx, understand of her history, and how, as a writer, did she make use of that story?

My mother and Hellman were of the same generation (my mother the elder by seven years) but born worlds apart—Hellman in New Orleans, my mother in a small village in the Ukraine. Yet, they had come to the same political conclusions about the Soviet Union. Hellman's politics, which took up a large space in her life, were of great interest to me. And so, of course, was her work, which I have read with attention, the plays and the memoirs, in which she is both revealed and hidden.

About those memoirs, for which I believe Hellman will ultimately be remembered: She began writing them in her mid-sixties. She was at the right time of life for such an enterprise—the tumult of youth passed, perspective and wisdom presumably gained, the infirmities of age still below the horizon. She had rich material to recollect. She knew everyone, had done everything, had been everywhere. She had forged a brilliant career on Broadway and in Hollywood. She had traveled widely and had stories of political and historical interest, particularly her experiences in prewar Germany, in Civil War Spain, in wartime Moscow. Her life had been, and remained, enviable: she had beautiful houses and beautiful clothes; her parties were glamorous, her friends were renowned, she had had more than her share of love affairs, and a public political life. There was also the matter of the persona that she had cultivated throughout her life: that of a tough-talking, truth-telling dame, a let-the-chips-fall-where-they-may sort of woman. What might her readers learn about the relation of the person to the persona? What would Hellman finally make of herself and her time?

Hellman worked steadily on her memoirs. Between 1969

and 1976, three volumes—*An Unfinished Woman, Pentimento,* and *Scoundrel Time*—were published, each to initial acclaim. In 1977, "Julia," one of the stories from *Pentimento,* was made into an Academy Award–winning movie starring Jane Fonda and Vanessa Redgrave. The memoirs and the movie brought Hellman to the attention of a new generation, and her reputation, which had faded somewhat during the sixties, was restored to high shine.

And then, just as the ailments of old age began to accumulate, Hellman's reputation hit slippery ground. Her description of her courageous, lonely stand before HUAC, as she had written about it in *Scoundrel Time,* was challenged by her contemporaries as historically distorted and self-serving. The celebrated story of her dear friend Julia, for whom she had virtually risked capture by the Nazis, seemed to have no basis in fact. In 1980, the writer, and Hellman's political adversary, Mary McCarthy, while being interviewed on television, said that Lillian Hellman lied with every word she wrote. In a fury, Hellman sued McCarthy, and in so doing opened her entire life to scrutiny, so that even the seemingly innocent stories of her childhood looked suspicious on second reading.

With McCarthy's words in mind, one re-reads, for example, a story Hellman tells of an incident that took place in New Orleans when she was a girl of about eleven years old: One evening Lillian's beloved black nurse, Sophronia, takes her to the movies. Afterward, they board a streetcar to go home. With the deliberate intention of challenging segregation, young Lillian takes a seat just behind the driver and pulls Sophronia down next to her.

> "Back," said the driver.
> I held so tight to her arm that [Sophronia] couldn't move.
> He said, "Get back in the car. You know better than this."

I said, my voice high with fright, "We won't. We won't move. This lady is better than you are—"[3]

As it was surely meant to do, the incident speaks very well for Hellman's early and lifelong sense of justice. And we must admit that the story might have happened as Hellman tells it. There is no one alive—not Sophronia, not the bus driver nor any of the nameless passengers—to say that forty years before Rosa Parks refused to move to the back of the bus, little, white Lillian Hellman didn't have the same idea. But to read the story knowing that Hellman's reputation for honesty had come under question, that in her old age the persona and character she had worked so hard to construct was beginning to crack, is to see something very different than the author intended.

In her memoirs, Hellman tells of another childhood incident. In this one she runs away from home and stays out all night, terrifying her parents. "From that day on," Hellman writes, "I knew my power over my parents ... [and] I found out something more useful and more dangerous: if you are willing to take the punishment, you are halfway through the battle."[4] Hellman offers this story as a key to her character. But surely she has left something out: the reader will search the pages of this story in vain for any indication that she was ever punished. In fact, her father, when he found her, treated her to a very large breakfast.

1

———◆•◆•◆———

The Hubbards of Bowden

BY THE time Lillian Florence Hellman was born in New Orleans in 1905, her once-burgeoning family in Demopolis, Alabama, had dwindled to a great-aunt or two, and a few cousins of the once-removed degree. Hellman seldom visited the town where her maternal great-grandfather, Isaac Marx, had settled in 1840, but Demopolis held the power of myth for her.

Hellman wrote two plays based on the Marx family. The first was *The Little Foxes*, produced in 1939. Seven years later she wrote a prequel, *Another Part of the Forest*. From time to time both plays are revived, and not long ago I went to see an off-Broadway production of *Another Part of the Forest*.

The time is 1880. Marcus Hubbard, a vigorous man in his sixties, is the tyrannical patriarch of his family. He has an unhappy wife, Lavinia, two grasping, resentful sons, Ben and Oscar, whom he keeps on a very short leash; and there is Regina, a beautiful, intelligent, manipulative girl, Marcus's best-loved child. The family lives in Bowden, a small town somewhere in Alabama. The Civil War is only fifteen years in the past, and it is the pervasive background to the action of the play.

Marcus's neighbors have been ruined by the war, their stately plantation houses are crumbling, the fields once worked by their slaves are filled with weeds. But the Hubbards are rich. They live in a grand house. Marcus, a remarkably cultivated man, is able to indulge his passions for books, for music, for ancient Greek history. It seems that Marcus has somehow profited from the Civil War. And, although Marcus has lived in Bowden for forty years, he and his family are pariahs; no one of any social importance will visit his house. And we learn that the Hubbards are in danger from the Klan:

"You have good reason to know," the aristocratic Colonel Isham says to Marcus, "there's not a man in this county wouldn't like to swing up anybody called Hubbard." So Marcus has a secret; the action of the play will revolve around its revelation.

Marcus's children are also plotting against him. They want his money. Regina, who is having a secret love affair with John Bagtry, a penniless ex-Confederate soldier, wants money to run away with Bagtry. Oscar, the middle child, a feckless dimwit, works for Marcus in the family store where he is paid a paltry wage. Oscar is desperate for money so that he can marry Laurette, a prostitute, and live with her in New Orleans. Ben, the eldest of the Hubbard children at thirty-five, is, like Regina, very intelligent. He also works for Marcus, and is badly paid. He wants money to make himself independently wealthy by investing in the industries that are coming to the new South. And Ben wants more than Marcus's money; he wants to humiliate and defeat his all-powerful father. Even Lavinia, Marcus's wife, who had been loyal to her husband until now, wants money to get away from her husband. She wants to start a school for colored children in the "piney woods."

Except for the hapless Lavinia, who goes to colored churches all the time, the Hubbards, father and children, are venal, amoral, wicked. They will say and do anything to get what they want—Marcus to keep his wealth and power, his children to wrest it from him.

It becomes clear that Marcus has made his money by profiteering on the sale of salt to a defeated and starving South. This is enough for his neighbors to hate him, but there is something worse. In consequence of his avarice, Marcus has inadvertently led Union soldiers to the hiding place of a group of Confederate soldiers. The Southern boys were massacred. The citizens of Bowden suspect that Marcus was responsible for the massacre, but they cannot prove it. Only Lavinia has the proof. She has kept Marcus's secret for fifteen years. But now, desperate to leave her husband, she will betray him.

Another Part of the Forest opened at Broadway's Fulton Theatre, in November 1946. Hellman had a lot riding on the play. She had not only written it, but for the first time she had directed her own play, and she was not entirely happy about its reception. Some critics were enthusiastic. The *New York Daily Mirror* critic called the play "magnetic and lusty theatre." Brooks Atkinson disagreed in the *New York Times;* he thought the Hubbards were "horrible" and called the play "demonic . . . a witch's brew of blackmail, insanity, cruelty, theft, torture, insult, drunkenness, with a trace of incest thrown in for good measure." Eric Bentley thought it was "a pretty good play" but hollow at its center: "At some of the most hideous moments in Miss Hellman's play the audience laughs and is not entirely wrong in doing so . . . *Another Part of the Forest* is Grand Guignol in the guise of realism."[1]

Another Part of the Forest displays Hellman's essential talent: Her dialogue is venomous and clever, there is not a dull or wasted moment in the play. At the end, every strand of the plot is tied up tightly. The action seems inevitable, no element of plot or character could be otherwise. It is only when the curtain comes down, and there is a moment to take a breath, that a viewer may find some room in the tightly constructed story to wonder what it was all about.

What does Hellman want us to understand about these venomous, rapacious Hubbards? Are they southerners? If so, they behave quite differently from the other southerners in the play, who are nothing if not genteel and honorable even in their poverty and defeat. And if the Hubbards are outsiders, where did they come from?

There is also something puzzling about the moral balance of *Another Part of the Forest*. The Civil War is little more than a plot device; the evil of slavery is barely mentioned. Hellman's sympathy lies with the characters who were the backbone of the antebellum South. With Colonel Isham, who no doubt once owned slaves himself; he is a gentleman of principle. He despises Marcus Hubbard, but he comes to warn him of danger. Hellman is remarkably tender to Regina's lover, John Bagtry, who fought with passionate idealism for the Old South's "way of life." Bagtry was happiest, he says, as a Confederate soldier; he is even planning to go to Brazil to join the slave owners there in their fight for the continuation of slavery. John's cousin Birdie, made destitute by the destruction of slavery, has fine manners, a sweet nature, and a concern for the welfare of the people whom she once owned. Only the Hubbards are without a saving grace.

Hellman made no claim that the Hubbards sprang to her imagination from thin air. She acknowledged that their origin lay with her own maternal relatives, the Marx-Newhouse family. As a girl she had listened intently to their dinner table conversations: intense, lively, competitive discussions about money and business deals. The family table talk provided her with the source material for the slashing, angry wit and rapaciousness of the Hubbards: Money—how it is made, how it is used, how the love of it is the root of social and personal evil is the idea that powered her play. It was surely no accident that when Hellman began work on *Forest*, she had recently returned from a ten-week stay in the Soviet Union, a country with which she and Hammett had long been in sympathy. And as Hellman, with Hammett's guidance, worked on *Forest*, it is not far-fetched to think that she experienced an epiphany, finding in her family the source of her politics. For relations between the Hubbard family, as Hellman has rendered them, can be read as an almost direct translation of a passage from the *Communist Manifesto*:

> The bourgeoisie has torn away from the family its sentimental veil, and has reduced the family relation to a mere money relation.

If she has dealt with the central theme of money in *Another Part of the Forest*, Hellman leaves some mystery around the matter of Marcus's origins. He has lived in Bowden for forty years, half of that time before the Civil War, before he had the opportunity to amass his fortune at the expense of the southern cause. Yet we have the distinct impression that the Hubbards have always been pariahs.

"It is hard to think of Regina and her brothers as Southern," Elizabeth Hardwick, herself a southerner, wrote after seeing a production of the earlier Hubbard play, *The Little Foxes*, in 1967. "There is little of the rural in their nature or in their cunning."[2]

Hellman leaves it to Laurette, the prostitute whom Oscar wants to marry, to reveal Marcus's origin:

"*Pretend?*" says Laurette to Oscar, "Pretend I'm as good as anybody called Hubbard. . . . I'm as good as piney wood crooks."

There is no town called Bowden, of course, but Demopolis is at the edge of a large area of the country, which stretches from southeast Texas to Florida, and is called the Piney Woods.

On October 31, 1865, when the Civil War had just ended, a Special Correspondent to the *New York Times* filed a story about his visit to the Piney Woods. He describes a benighted place, grimly destitute, where the people are illiterate, where they have never heard of, much less seen, a newspaper or a book:

> Throughout the Southern portion of Alabama, upon both sides of the river, is what is known as the "piney-woods" country. It is one of the most barren sections I have ever seen. Neither corn nor cotton will grow to any extent. Sweet potatoes are the chief product, and this vegetable, and bacon, with a little corn bread, form the bill of fare morning, noon, night, all the year round. These people are scattered all through these "piney-woods," and live in log huts which in a way protect them from the . . . violent storms of wind and rain which howl through this barren waste during certain periods of the year. Oh, how I pity these poor beings who have been the recipients of untold woes and unheard of sufferings during the long, long years of African slavery . . . let us not in our endeavors to elevate the black man, forget these poor whites who have suffered more and enjoyed less, than their colored brethren in bondage.

So Marcus is poor white trash from the backwoods. Hellman gives him one speech to make a bid for the sympathy of the audience:

> At nine years old I was carrying water for two bits a week. I took the first dollar I ever had and went to the paying library to buy a card. When I was twelve I was working out in the fields, and that same year I taught myself Latin and French. At fourteen I was driving mules all day and most of the night, but that was the year I learned my Greek, read my classics, taught myself.

The world is full of autodidacts, and no doubt some have emerged from the Piney Woods. But how often does it happen that an illiterate boy, a boy from an environment where hunger and ignorance are the constant conditions of life, where there are no books or talk of books, or of ancient civilizations; how often does it happen that such a young boy steps out of the piney woods, and uses his first saved dollar to buy a library card? Wherever did he get the idea that books and music and ancient languages were valuable things?

Marcus's speech might come more believably from someone of another origin. Someone who, for instance, comes from people with a centuries-long history of being outsiders wherever they happen to settle. Those who have learned, from lack of other opportunities, to live by buying, selling, and lending, the methods by which Marcus has, even if pitilessly, amassed his fortune. These are people who prize literacy even when they are barely literate, who know quite a lot about the long arc of history even as they have been confined to ghettos, been oppressed, exiled, and persecuted. These people, when social restrictions loosen, are known to strive for education for themselves, but especially for their children.

Isaac Marx, who died five years before Hellman's birth, was a Jew who had emigrated from Bavaria in 1840 and had settled in small-town Demopolis, Alabama. Among his many children born in Demopolis were Hellman's grandmother, Sophie, and her daughter, Julia, who became Hellman's mother.

It was not in Hellman's gift to create a Shylock of the South. Nor was she inclined, as Clifford Odets was, to write empathetically about New York Jews in their poverty and striving. Hellman preferred to write for a wide Broadway audience. And unlike Odets, she felt neither empathy nor sympathy for her Hubbards. Quite the opposite. It was her antagonism to her characters that gives her play its power. And, then, of course, if you have written a play about people who are manipulative money-grubbers, whose gains are ill-gotten, it was not possible, certainly not in 1946, to identify them as Jews.

2

The Marxes of Demopolis

DEMOPOLIS IS a pretty river town deep in Alabama, about 140 miles north of Mobile, and not very far from the Mississippi border. Tourists come to these parts to admire three local plantation houses—Gaineswood, Lyon Hall, and Bluff Hall—which have been beautifully preserved and restored. Visitors are charmed, also, by the nineteenth-century downtown buildings, which have also been preserved and are in commercial use, and by the setting of Demopolis, itself, built on a chalk cliff high above the junction of two rivers, the Tombigbee and the Black Warrior, which meet to flow down to the Gulf of Mexico.

Should you ever visit Demopolis and express an interest in Lillian Hellman, you will be introduced to a woman who will show you an old white linen tablecloth. After more than a century of use the cloth is threadbare and torn in places; in angled bright light you can barely make out the central design of an eagle's head. The owner of the cloth will tell you that it has been in her family since the 1840s, when it was given to her great-grandmother, Dorothy Stewart, by Lillian Hellman's great-grandfather, the peddler boy, Isaac Marx; it was a trade for a meal and a night's lodging in Mrs. Stewart's house several miles out on the Jefferson Road. This little story, and the decrepit cloth, is the only tangible evidence of Isaac Marx's peddling days. The cloth should have seen the rag bin years ago, but this is the South, and antebellum artifacts carry a lot of weight.

Isaac Marx, Lillian Hellman's great-grandfather, was born in Bavaria. The year of his birth was 1825, or 1824, depending on which census you look at. He gave the name of his small town in the Rhine Pfalz region of Bavaria that first records the presence of Jews in 906. The records of subsequent centuries are filled with the long, often dark, history of the Jews of central Europe, but Isaac was born in the first quarter of the nineteenth century, a relatively benign time, when, in many parts of Germany, Jewish children were allowed to attend general schools, and when Jews were granted citizenship, if a special class of citizenship, distinguished by a "Jew tax." In many towns authorities controlled their Jewish demographics by allowing only the eldest son of a Jewish family to marry, and then only if the family could pay a large marriage tax. In some regions, a boy grown to manhood in a particular town was allowed to remain in his hometown only if he replaced a Jew who had recently died.

We know almost nothing about Isaac Marx's family. We don't know how long the Marxes had lived in this part of the world, not how they made a living, not how many siblings Isaac had, although they seem to have been numerous. We can assume that the family was poor, as most Jews living in the German countryside were in the nineteenth century. But by the early and mid-1800s Jews could more readily leave

Europe, and especially once steamship technology shrunk the Atlantic. Those families who could raise the fare began to send their sons away. Between 1820 and 1880, a quarter of a million young Jews, most of them from Germany, made the voyage to America. In some unrecorded month in 1840, fifteen-year-old Isaac Marx stepped off a ship in a port city on the Gulf of Mexico. He had relatives in Mobile, and Mobile would be a constant reference point in his life, the city where he would marry, where he would live for a time, and where, in 1900, he was buried.

Not long after his arrival in Mobile, Isaac bought a peddler's pack. He would have had no experience in farming; Jews in Europe had not been allowed to own land. They might be skilled as tailors, or as tanners; more likely the immigrants knew trading, buying, and selling, the basic tools of capitalism. In Europe, the Jewish economy "rode on the backs of peddlers," as one historian has put it. In parts of Europe, in the nineteenth century, Jews were allowed to sell no more merchandise than they could carry. The skills required for peddling—buy cheap, sell at a small profit—were transferable to any part of the world.[1] If Jewish merchants had once traveled the Silk Road in caravans of camels, they could manage on the roads of the rural South.

Peddling offered the poor immigrant an entry into the economic life of the new country.[2] When Isaac arrived in Mobile in 1840, a community of Jewish merchants was already established, many of whom would supply a peddler on credit. In the pre-industrial antebellum South, with farms, plantations, and settlements set far apart, with few stores, primitive roads, and railroads that extended to few places, and river systems where steam boats took you just so far, a woman who longed to curtain her windows against the dark might travel a half day to reach a store that sold cloth. But along comes Isaac Marx, walking through the sparsely settled nineteenth-century countryside, with notions and curtains and tablecloths in his pack.

At this point it is unlikely that Isaac spoke much English. Not that a peddler needs many words. When he spreads his goods before the lady of the house, it is sufficient to say: *Lady buy?* And when night falls, *Can I sleep here?* More important to a successful enterprise is the ability to achieve profit, limit loss, and calculate credit and interest.

Peddling requires youth and health. A peddler walks all day in all weathers, carrying a heavy pack. Persistence and courage are important qualities. He has to face the occasional slammed door, the ferocious dog, insults, boys who throw stones. Then he has to return to those places. And he has to keep his goal in mind, which is not to peddle forever, but to make enough profit from his efforts so that, first, he can pay off his supplier and buy new goods; beyond that, to save enough money to bring family from Europe, then to find a place to settle and open a business, to meet a suitable girl, marry, and have children.

Isaac may have been the first Jew his customers had ever seen. In the South, this was not the liability it would have been in other parts of the country. Southerners already had their Other. Isaac was white. True, he was a foreigner with a strange accent, but this could work to his advantage. He was not expected to understand local customs. If he took his goods into slave quarters, he knew no better. He could go into the grand houses of plantation owners to sell second-hand clothes for their slaves and into the shacks of poor white farmers. He could sleep wherever he was allowed, even with slaves. If he was respectful to his customers, if his goods were not shoddy, if he offered credit on reasonable terms, he would be given special orders to fill, and welcomed on his return.[3]

It is simply astonishing to think of the great fortunes that were built on the nickel-and-dime profits of peddling. Great banking fortunes and mercantile fortunes—the Lehman brothers, the Seligman brothers, the Rich brothers—German Jewish immigrants all, who began by peddling in the antebellum South.

Having brothers seems to have been a predicate for success. There was an understanding among Jewish families who sent a son to America that the boy who arrived first would prepare the ground for the next one. Two brothers worked together and profits doubled; a third brother was sent for. Isaac seems to have been the third brother. His brother Henry, eight years his senior, was already in Mobile when he arrived; and his brother Lehman, three years his elder, was also in the area.

Marengo County, of which Demopolis is the principal town, is the heart of the black belt, that wide swath of dark, fertile soil in which cotton grew so well. Inevitably, the term black belt also came to refer to the County's population of slaves. By 1850, at the height of the County's prosperity, the ratio of slaves to whites was almost three to one. In 1853 a local editor wrote about the basis of his County's prosperity: "Marvelous accounts had gone forth of the fertility of [Marengo County's] virgin lands. . . . The productions of the soil were commanding a price remunerating to slave labor as it had never been remunerated before."[4] By 1860, the ratio of black to white had risen to seventy-eight percent of the County's population.[5]

As Marengo County prospered, so did Demopolis, which was perfectly situated to serve a cotton economy. From Demopolis, cotton grown in the black belt could be stored in the town's riverbank warehouses, then shipped downriver to arrive in Mobile thirty hours later; and from Mobile, shipped on to the garment centers of New York and London. From Mobile, all manner of goods and people came upriver to Demopolis.

Isaac Marx was the first Jew to settle in Demopolis. By the 1850s, a number of others had opened businesses in town, and by 1858 there were enough Jews to form a congregation, although Demopolis would never have a permanent rabbi, and a temple was not built until 1893.

Isaac set up his first dry goods store in 1844, a small wooden structure in which he probably also lived. The store did well enough so that he was able to buy property on the more central corner of Market and Capitol Streets. There, he built a larger general merchandise store. This building no longer exists, but on the corner of Washington and Walnut Streets, you can still see the original Marx Brothers Banking Company, built in 1885, and still functioning as a bank. Just around the corner from the bank is a livery stable (now a law office) built in 1898; in very faded black paint the building is identified as "Marx Mules and Wagons." Both the bank and livery stable were established for, and run by, Isaac's sons. The Marxes, father and sons, were enterprising men, alert to economic opportunity, ready to seize the main chance.

By the time Hellman wrote her plays about the Hubbard family, she was in her mid-thirties. Her opinions about history and politics were firmly settled. If the Hubbards were little more than symbols of the destructive power of money, we know that at the beginning of her life the Hellmans were poor relations of the Marxes. "Shabby poor," Lillian wrote. Prideful child that she was, prideful woman that she became, the status of poor relation galled her. She resented her mother's family, resented her awe of them; she was jealous of their wealth, and shamed by the disrespect they showed her much-loved father. Max Hellman may have been as handsome and charming and witty as his daughter said he was (although photographs show him to be a homely, pudgy man), but from the Marxes' viewpoint, he was a failure as a businessman, which was the talent they valued. Max Hellman did not like the Marxes any more than his daughter did. And Hellman's conflicting feelings, as she wrote in her memoirs, "made me into an angry child."[6] Anger followed her all the way into womanhood. The intense energy of her Hubbard plays is fueled by anger, tightly controlled by the artist she was.

Hellman tells us that "after *The Little Foxes* was written and put away, this conflict was to grow less important, as indeed the picture of my mother's family was to grow dim and almost fade away."[7] But this is not quite true. Her mother's family remained vivid enough so that seven years after *Foxes*, she gathered the Hubbards for *Another Part of the Forest*. And they must have remained in her mind for some years after that when she frequently spoke of her intention to make a trilogy of the Hubbard plays. Money, the getting of it, the having of it, the spending and lending of it, her attraction to and disdain for the rich, lasted all through Hellman's life. It made her behave in some peculiar ways.

For Isaac Marx, born eighty years before his great-granddaughter, money was neither complicated nor symbolic. Had he been a reader of the Talmud, he would have come across the following passage:

> Nothing is harder to bear than poverty, because he who is crushed by poverty is like one to whom all the troubles of the world cling and upon whom all the curses of Deuteronomy have descended. If all other troubles were placed on one side and poverty on the other, poverty would outweigh them all.[8]

Isaac does not seem to have been a particularly religious man, but he would not have needed the Talmud to teach him about poverty. He had seen real poverty, he had known it; he had managed to escape it, and evidently meant never to know it again.

Isaac Marx makes his first appearance as a resident of Demopolis in the Federal Census of 1850. The information in the census is scant. He is listed as a merchant, twenty-five years old, born in Germany; the only other listed member of his household at this time is his twenty-eight-year-old brother, Lehman, also a merchant. Both men are bachelors.

By 1853, Isaac was married. His bride, Amelia Weidenreich, was a girl from the Rhine Pfalz region of Bavaria.[9] Isaac was twenty-eight, Amelia eighteen. The wedding took place in Mobile, and since there is no sign of any member of Amelia's family in Mobile or in Demopolis, and since Amelia came from a town in Bavaria close to Isaac's own, it would seem likely that the match was arranged between their families, and Amelia sent over for the wedding. The couple may have been cousins; Hellman mentions a marriage between cousins in *The Little Foxes*. But whether or not they were related, they were strangers to each other; had they ever seen each other before, Amelia would have been no more than five years old.

Very soon Amelia was pregnant. A year after her marriage, she gave birth to a girl, Sophie, Hellman's grandmother. From the age of eighteen until she was forty-seven, Amelia gave birth on an average of every other year, producing a total of ten children. Two babies did not survive childhood; a son disappears from the records in early adulthood, presumably dead of disease or accident.

The 1860 Census, the last taken before the Civil War, shows us that during the 1850s Isaac had become quite a substantial citizen. He was now head of a household of seven people including himself, his wife, and their four children. Moses Marx, a young man from Bavaria, perhaps Isaac's youngest brother, also lived with them and clerked in Isaac's store.

In the same census Isaac, when asked the value of his real and personal property, gave the figure of $23,000. This made him far from the wealthiest man in town—the great wealth was held by the planters—but he was equally far from the poorest. His real property would have included the value of his store, and of the house which he had by then built for his family. Some fraction of his personal property—in the vicinity of four or five thousand dollars—inhered in the value of his five slaves, who were listed only by sex and age. The Marx family owned a forty-year-old black male; a black female of the same age; a twenty-eight-year-old black female; a thirteen-year-old mulatto female; and a black female child, seven years old.[10]

In 1860, a quarter of all southern families owned slaves. "Whatever the ultimate affirmations of the Jewish religious tradition . . . individual Jews are strongly aware of the need to live in this world from day to day," the critic Robert Warshow wrote in the late 1940s.[11] Living day to day in the South, Jews accepted slavery as the law of the land: "The law of the land is the law [for the Jews]," the Talmud says. Indeed, the law of the land was also accepted by those who had most reason to object to it—free southern blacks who owned slaves, as many did.[12]

The law of the land was different in the North, and most northern Jews opposed secession and slavery. Overt antisemitism was also more prevalent in the North than in the South. The fervent abolitionist William Lloyd Garrison, editor of the *Liberator,* saw no contradiction between abhorrence of slavery and hatred of Jews, referring to a northern Jewish judge as "the miscreant Jew," a "Shylock," a "descendant of the monsters who nailed Jesus to the cross."[13] Had it not been for the presence of African slaves, antisemitism in the South would have been much closer to the surface. Jews, who had done so well in the South, feared nothing more than the stirring of that pot.

When Alabama seceded from the Union in January 1861, there were fewer than 25,000 Jews living in the southern states. Between 2,000 and 3,000 of them served in the Confederate armies.[14] Lillian Hellman's family provided two soldiers to the Confederacy: her paternal grandfather, Bernard Hellman, who served as a quartermaster in Florida;[15] Isaac Marx is first listed as a private in the Canebrake Legion of the Confederate Cavalry and then, in 1863, as a quartermaster.[16]

In *Another Part of the Forest*, Marcus Hubbard runs the Union blockade to bring back salt. In the few records that exist of Isaac Marx's activities as a quartermaster, there is no mention of salt, but there are some receipts for a horse he supplied to the Confederate Army for $800, some packing boxes for bacon, and forty-four bushels of something illegible, for which he was paid a total of $345. Of course there would have been many more transactions than the few that have survived and many transactions for which a record was never made. Some may have had to do with salt, or with the black market in cotton. General Ulysses Grant, convinced that Jews were responsible for the black market in cotton, issued the notorious General Order No. 11 in 1862, for the expulsion of all Jews from the areas of Tennessee, Mississippi, and Kentucky occupied by the Union. The order was quickly rescinded by Lincoln. But many men, including Jews, profited during the Civil War. And, in fact, Isaac Marx was a much richer man in the late 1860s than he was before the war began.

For some reason, at about the time the war ended, Isaac moved his family to Mobile. His son Julius was born there in 1865; two more children followed.[17] In 1868, he built a townhouse in Mobile, an elegant house, typical of city architecture, with bay windows and shutters, a cast iron veranda, white marble fireplaces, a small formal garden, and imported French wallpaper. We know so much about this house because much later it was dismantled and re-erected for use on the campus of the University of South Alabama.[18] The Mobile Census of 1870 shows him living in this house with Amelia and seven children. The value of Isaac's real estate had risen to $100,000, and his personal worth to $50,000, although this is probably a low estimate; no one tells the census taker the whole truth about his finances.

In the years between 1860 and 1870, while the economy of the Old South crumbled, Isaac Marx made a fortune. Probably he bought land; the old plantations, now without slave labor to work them, were going cheap. No doubt he rented the land to freedmen to work, and took a share, a large share, of their crops. He was also a money lender.

Isaac returned to Demopolis in about 1872. There is no suggestion that scandal was attached to his name. The newly formed Demopolis Board of Trade elected him as a member.[19] Isaac continued to be involved in his various businesses. When a temple was finally built in Demopolis in 1893, Isaac lit the perpetual light.

In 1875 Amelia gave birth for the last time, to another boy, Henry. Ten years later Isaac built the bank for his eldest sons, Jacob and Edward; in 1898, he built the Marx Livery Stable, for the younger boys, Julius and Henry. His children had been educated and were prepared to take their place in the world. Specifically, we know that his son Julius graduated from college in Mobile with a master's degree, and we can assume that the other Marx boys had been educated as well.[20]

The children began to marry. In 1876, Sophie, the eldest of the Marx children, married Leonard Newhouse, who had come from Cincinnati to be a merchant in Demopolis. The Newhouses had four children, a boy and three girls. Julia, Lillian Hellman's mother, was their second child, born in 1879.

And the older generation began to die. Amelia in 1898, and Isaac in 1900, at the age of seventy-five. Only two of the Marx children, Julius and Henry, remained in Demopolis to live out their lives.

In 1897, Leonard Newhouse died of syphilis. Sophie Marx Newhouse found herself a wealthy, and still-young widow. Like Regina Hubbard in *The Little Foxes*, Sophie longed for big city life; unlike Regina, she was not hampered by lack of money. She took her four unmarried children and left Demopolis, going first to Cincinnati, her late husband's birthplace, and soon after to New Orleans. There, to her dismay, her daughter, Julia, met and married Max Hellman.

Sophie was displeased with the match. Max did not seem to be, nor was he, a man of force and business acumen. But Julia was given her dowry, and Max opened a shoe manufacturing business. In 1905, the couple's only child was born, a girl, named Lillian Florence. The new family lived first with Sophie Newhouse, and then with Max Hellman's sisters, Jenny and Hannah, who ran a boarding house.

By 1910 Sophie Marx Newhouse and her children were in New York. Sophie's brother Jacob Marx left Demopolis to join her in the city. The Newhouses took apartments in the grand, newly built Ansonia Hotel on Broadway between 73rd and 74th Streets, which featured tower apartments and oval living rooms. In that day, as it still is today, the Ansonia was an architectural gem of the Upper West Side.

Max Hellman's shoe business in New Orleans failed. Sometime around 1910, the Hellman family, too, moved to New York. Everything about their residence in the city was at first tentative. They lived in a boarding house. Max worked as a traveling shoe salesman, and Julia and Lillian often traveled with him. For some years Lillian was sent to New Orleans for part of the school year. Eventually the family settled, taking an apartment in a solidly middle-class building on 95th Street near Riverside Drive; still their quarters were a great deal less luxurious than those the Marxes occupied at the Ansonia.[21]

3

Two Jewish Girls

ONE EVENING in Hollywood, in 1935, a dinner party was given to honor Gertrude Stein. Among the invited guests were Charlie Chaplin and Dashiell Hammett, both of whom Stein had asked to meet. Dashiell Hammett brought Lillian Hellman along as his date.

It is a little difficult to picture Lillian Hellman and Gertrude Stein in the same room at the same time. Something like trying to hold two opposing thoughts. These women do not belong together. Surely, they must be of different eras and different worlds. But, in fact, they were both American girls, Jewish girls, only a generation apart, and they both knew something of life in the South.

Hellman was thirty in 1935, short and slender, with a large bosom, good legs that she played up, and always elegantly dressed and coiffed. Stein was sixty, also short, but unapologetically fat, which exempted her from fashion; few people knew anything about her legs.

One can almost imagine that these physical differences between Hellman and Stein translated directly to the page: in Hellman's tightly woven plots and precisely pointed sentences; in Stein's loose, verbose, repetitious, plotless meanderings, in English, yes, but not as it is generally written or spoken. (Stein's brother, Leo, who was bitter about his sister's success, thought that she simply couldn't write any better.[1])

More than appearance and writing styles differentiated the women. One preferred men, the other loved women. Each woman held extreme political views that the other would have abhorred. The social and cultural circumstances of one would have been deeply uncongenial to the other. At the moment they met, however, they were alike in being new American celebrities: Hellman, freshly acclaimed for her first play, *The Children's Hour*; and Stein, already famous for being Gertrude Stein, was making a lecture tour of America with her first popular success, *The Autobiography of Alice B. Toklas*.

It is too much to say that Hellman and Stein became acquainted that evening. Stein paid no attention to Hellman. It was Dashiell Hammett who interested her and whose work she admired. (Hellman didn't forget the snub, and many years later she told an interviewer a story about that evening to Stein's disadvantage.[2])

This meeting between the two women was the first and the last, and with no significance for their lives. It is also insignificant, if not uninteresting, that Stein and Hellman, at different times, had a relationship with Ernest Hemingway in which sex hovered at the edges. "I always wanted to fuck her and she knew it," Hemingway wrote of Stein long after their friendship was over.[3] For her part, Hellman recounted a night spent with Hemingway in Paris. It was 1937; Hellman was in a deep drunken sleep in her hotel room when she was awakened by someone pounding on her door. Hemingway! What could a man want at that hour? But, no. he was carrying the proofs of his new novel *To Have and Have Not* and eager only for Hellman's opinion. Hellman read through the night, making discerning comments that seemed to annoy Hemingway. When dawn broke, Hemingway took his leave, but not before offering Hemingwayesque thanks: "I wish I could sleep with you," he said, "but I can't because there's somebody else. I hope you understand."[4]

Between Stein and Hemingway we can be sure that nothing happened, apart from that frisson that made their friendship, as long as it lasted, more interesting. But between Hellman and Hemingway, who can say? When Hellman got back to New York, she let it be known that she had been one of Hemingway's girls in Paris, and was "very bitter over him."[5] But digressions aside, what on earth is Gertrude Stein doing in Lillian Hellman's story?

If I found it surprising to find these birds of such different feather in the same room, how much more surprising it was to learn that they had so much in common that they might have been hatched from the same clutch. Like Hellman's great-grandfather, Isaac Marx, the Steins had fled impoverished lives in Bavaria. In 1841, a year after Isaac Marx landed in Mobile, the Steins landed in Baltimore with four young sons. In Baltimore, they were met by Meyer, their eldest son, who, like Isaac Marx, had earned the money to send for them by peddling old clothes.

In time, Meyer Stein opened a dry goods store in Baltimore. His younger brothers joined him in the enterprise, including his brother Daniel, who would be Gertrude's father. During the 1850s, the store grew into a successful clothing manufacturing business. Since Maryland was a border state, when

Civil War broke out the Steins were able to obtain contracts to manufacture military uniforms for the Union side.

It's possible that the maternal side of Gertrude Stein's family, the Keysers, were slave owners at some point. The Keysers had been settled in Baltimore since the 1820s, and they were in favor of secession from the Union. Gertrude's maternal uncle, Solomon, fought for the Confederacy.

The Stein family was divided on the question of secession. Daniel Stein sympathized with the Union. In 1862, Daniel and one of his younger brothers left Baltimore for Pittsburgh, where they set up a branch of the family business. The 1870 Census lists the worth of Daniel Stein's real and personal property at the considerable sum of $60,000.[6]

Many German-Jewish families have stories similar to the Marxes and the Steins: impoverishment and oppression in the Old Country; peddling in the New World; hard work, and a rise to riches. Few of these families, however, produced such writing daughters, girls who grew into exceptionally distinctive women, girls with enough self-assurance to live without the protection of marriage, and to follow their own inclinations.

Stein's self-confidence was striking: it was "outlandish confidence," as Elizabeth Hardwick observed, "confidence and its-not-too-gradual ascent into egoism."[7] Stein's powerful sense of herself feels deeply organic, while Hellman's often seems like bravado. Whatever the nature of their confidence, neither of these women ever faltered in her course.

How did they get that way? In women, self-confidence is often based on beauty, but no one can accuse either of these girls of trading on her looks. Money in the family can be reassuring. Gertrude grew up a rich girl, in full knowledge that she would be provided for. Lillian had to earn her money, but her mother and grandmother had grown up rich, and while Lillian may have described herself as "shabby poor," she knew how rich people behaved; she had early coveted the wealth of her Marx relations. And, even as she condemned their methods of making money, and their obsession with money, in Hellman's plays about the Hubbards, she offers them no alternative: life without money is life without freedom.

Gertrude and Lillian also occupied a similar niche in their respective families. Gertrude was the baby, and as the baby, as Stein readily acknowledged, or boasted, "naturally I had privileges, the privilege of petting . . . there you are privileged, nobody can do anything but take care of you, that is the way I was and this is the way I still am."[8] Lillian was an only child, therefore forever the baby; if she sometimes emphasized the negative aspects of that status, she knew very well that she always got her way: "As an only child, you never have enough of anything. Because you're so spoiled all the time, and [getting a] lot has led to wishing for more."[9]

Hellman and Stein had these family circumstances in common, and now that we know a little more about the mechanisms of genetic inheritance, we can imagine that the qualities that brought two young impoverished men from Bavaria to America in the still-early nineteenth century were not lost; two and three generations down the line, their character traits may well have appeared in these fiercely willful and ambitious daughters, each of whom liked to think of herself as owing nothing to nobody.

Like Hellman, Stein used autobiographical material in her work. She often said that she had no imagination and couldn't make anything up. And like Hellman, she didn't concern herself with the Jewish aspect of her characters. Thornton Wilder, who was a friend and admirer of Stein's, wrote with some indignation to another mutual friend Alexander Woollcott: "Well, Gertrude Stein is a fine, big serene girl, is she? THEN why does she never mention [in *The Autobiography of Alice B. Toklas*] that she or Miss Toklas are Jewesses? And why in . . . "The Making of Americans" does she not mention that the family she is analyzing in such detail is a Jewish family. . . . It is possible to make books of a certain fascination if you scrupulously leave out the essential."[10]

Stein never denied being Jewish. In fact she took a quixotic pride in it. She had a theory that all geniuses (herself included) had Jewish blood; and so, because she considered him a genius, she was sure that Abraham Lincoln was partly Jewish. She had other very peculiar ideas. For instance, in 1934, while on her lecture tour of America, she urged that Hitler be awarded the Nobel Peace Prize. She told a reporter that Hitler, by "driving out the Jews and the democratic and Left elements [from Germany] . . . is driving out everything that conduces to activity. That means peace." Yet again, in 1938, she suggested that Hitler be considered for the Prize.[11] Whatever we think of Gertrude Stein as an artist, we might agree with the critic Robert Warshow, who wrote that "in politics she was stupid and uninformed."[12]

In 1940, as Germany occupied France, friends warned Stein and Toklas to leave the country immediately. For once, Stein was properly frightened; she almost fled. But in the end she did not. She had always felt specially charmed, and she could not believe that anything bad could happen to her. And, in fact, nothing bad did. She found a protector in Bernard Faÿ, a Nazi collaborator, who admired her, and whom she, in turn, admired. When Faÿ visited her at her country house in Bilignin, in France's Rhone Valley, the two friends spoke of many common interests, including Hitler, whom they thought a great man and compared to Napoleon.[13] "Faÿ successfully pleaded Stein's case with the Vichy authorities, and between 1941 and 1944, while the Vichy government, in collaboration with the Gestapo, deported 76,000 Jews to Nazi death camps, Stein and Toklas, and their pedigreed poodle, Basket, through

Faÿ's intervention, were supplied with enough coal and food rations to keep them alive, if a bit thinner, while they waited out the war in the French countryside.[14] "A Jew is a ghetto surrounded by Christians," Gertrude Stein once said, and so it proved in wartime France.[15]

Nor did Lillian Hellman ever deny being Jewish. She occasionally told interviewers that she liked being Jewish, even if, as she acknowledged, she had little sense of what that meant. In early 1940, she began to see a psychoanalyst, Dr. Gregory Zilboorg, who deserves and has his own chapter later. Hellman undertook analysis because she was concerned about her heavy drinking. According to an interview given by Zilboorg's widow after Hellman's death, the doctor noticed a couple of other problems; he hoped to cure his patient not only of alcoholism but of her chronic habit of lying, and of her antisemitism—"the deprecatory way with a curling lip she spoke of other Jews."[16]

It was no secret to her friends that Hellman often spoke contemptuously of Jews. "Get those Rappaports out of here," she might say of a group of people not authorized to be in a theater where she was working. The power boats bobbing in the harbor in front of her Martha's Vineyard property were "Jewish cocktail boats."[17] Walter Matthau, who starred in *My Mother, My Father and Me*, a play Hellman adapted, told her, as others did, that the play was antisemitic.[18] "I myself make very anti-Semitic remarks but I get upset if anyone else does," Hellman told an interviewer, the equivalent of saying, "Some of my best friends are Jewish," as indeed they were.[19] Although, again, like Gertrude Stein, no Jewish characters appeared in Hellman's plays, even when Jews would seem to be central to the plot.

A striking example is Hellman's anti-Fascist play *Watch on the Rhine*. First staged in 1941, her hero, Kurt Muller (most probably based on her friend, the Comintern agent Otto Katz, who was, in fact, Jewish, and on whom more later), is an Aryan German, and an exemplary anti-Fascist. Muller, we are told, fought for the Spanish Republic in the 1930s; in 1940, when the action of *Watch* is set, Muller is a leader of the anti-Nazi underground. We find him in Washington with his family, resting from the ordeals of being a hunted man in Europe. But soon he learns that he must return to Germany to try and rescue several of his captured comrades. This is a very dangerous undertaking, and it is unlikely that he will survive. We learn that Muller was forced to leave Germany in 1933, the year Hitler took power. Was this because he was:

> *A Jew?* one character asks of another.
> *No, I don't think so.*
> *Why did he have to leave Germany?*
> *Oh, I don't know, Teck. He's an anti-Nazi.*[20]

No one in this play is Jewish. If any of the comrades Kurt is going back to Germany to rescue is Jewish, he doesn't say so. It does seem a bit odd that Jews are barely mentioned in a play that specifically urges American liberals to rouse themselves to resist Hitler. There is a place in this play, as there was not in the Hubbard plays, for at least one heroic Jewish character, but there are none, even though such a character might carry some special moral weight given the message of Hellman's play.

In August 1939, when Hellman finished the first draft of *Watch on the Rhine*, she could not have known, no one did, the fate that would befall the Jews of Europe.[21] But she was not ignorant, no one was, of the Nazi hatred and persecution of Jews.

Both Gertrude Stein and Lillian Hellman were radicals. Stein was artistically as well as politically extreme. She was a radical conservative; during the decade of the Depression, Stein believed a hungry man was a lazy man. She was opposed to Franklin Roosevelt and the New Deal; she supported Franco in his attack on the Spanish Republic; she was for Hitler, at least in those of his policies she was so sure would lead to peace.

Hellman was traditional as an artist—she broke no new ground; she was on the far left side of the political divide. She admired Stalin and the Soviet Union; she believed in, and spoke publicly for, policies that were identical to those promulgated by the Communist Party. And so confident of their righteousness were both women, that events as they transpired barely ruffled their beliefs.

4

———◆•◆•◆———

Marriage

IT IS always interesting to ask about any couple: Why this particular man and woman? Why, to begin with, did Lillian Hellman marry Arthur Kober?

When Hellman met Kober, she was nineteen, still living with her parents in the walk-up apartment on West 95th Street, near Riverside Drive, where the family lived for most of the fifteen years since their arrival in New York. After her sophomore year Hellman had dropped out of New York University where she had been an indifferent student. She was restless and uncertain as young, inexperienced people are, but she was a bold girl. And she harbored vaguely literary ambitions. The diary in which she made sporadic entries between 1922 and 1925 records some high-flown adolescent musings: "I shall say—I am a seeker of the truth. I arrive at conclusions and then discard them. . . . I am essentially artificial in my struggle for the truth." About her active sex life: "Up to 2 hours we laid on the couch and should have had children but for many reasons didn't . . ."¹

Soon Hellman had a piece of good luck. At a party, a flirtatious conversation with a man who turned out to be a publishing executive led to a job with Boni and Liveright, an eminent publishing house with a stunning list of authors that included Theodore Dreiser, T. S. Eliot, Ernest Hemingway, and William Faulkner. Hellman's job was fairly menial, but she found herself in the vicinity of the twentieth-century's great writers and editors. As happens in life, one thing led to another, and a door into the world cracked open for her.

The Liveright office was friendly and informal. Hellman made some friends among the other young women working there. Among them, as she tells it in her memoirs, was a girl named "Alice" who "was already started on the road to Marxism that would lead her, as a student doctor, to be killed in the Vienna riots of 1934."² In her second memoir, Hellman's "Alice" became "Julia," and she lived on several more years. Whether or not there was an Alice-Julia, Hellman did meet Arthur Kober through her job at Liveright, probably at one of the parties thrown by the publisher. He was five years older than Hellman; they began a love affair and Hellman became pregnant. She had an abortion, but a few months after that, in December 1925, "I . . . left my job at Liveright's to marry Arthur Kober, who was a charming young man working as a theatre press agent and just beginning to write about his friends in the emerging Jewish-American lower middle class world."³

Hellman's parents liked Arthur Kober; everyone liked him. He was not handsome, but he was sweet, kind, and funny, if also insecure and subject to bouts of depression. He was crazy about Hellman, and she was fond of him, even loved him, while aware that he was not quite her ideal. As she wrote in her diary the year before they married: "I can't have the complete Don Juan because then I'd suspect something so I am growing quite content with a substitution."

Marriage to Kober offered many advantages. It got Hellman out of her parents' house, and gave her emotional protection. Kober was a promising writer; his connections in the literary and theatrical world would prove useful in getting Hellman work—first as a theatrical publicist, then as a script reader in Hollywood. She began writing book reviews and little stories that she knew were not very good. In 1928, when Kober got a temporary job editing a magazine in Paris, Hellman went with him for her first trip abroad.

Nor did marriage confine Hellman's sexual life. "In those days," she told an interviewer many years later, "we all thought we *should* be sexually liberated and acted as if we *were*, but we had deep uneasiness about sex too."[4] Not very long into her marriage, however uneasily, Hellman, in her own words, "began a history of remarkable men, often difficult, sometimes even dangerous."[5]

When Kober was offered a screenwriting contract in Hollywood, Hellman remained in New York for several months before joining him, and began a passionate love affair with a young man named David Cort, who went on to become a distinguished author and editor. The affair continued, on and off, for several years.[6] Kober was an insecure man and a compliant husband. He remained deeply attached to Hellman for the rest of his life, but when he later looked back at their marriage he saw her as "thoughtless, restless and idle."[7] And it is true that Lillian Kober, as she was known during the years of her marriage, did pretty much as she pleased. If it pleased her to be separate from Kober for months at a time, and it did, if it pleased her to have affairs, and it did, Kober had his own affairs, and hoped that in time the marriage would settle.[8]

In many ways the Kobers were mismatched: a headstrong, ambitious woman married to an appeasing, self-deprecating man is material for comedy, and certainly for conflict. "She could have had him for breakfast," Hellman's friend Talli Wyler said years later.[9] There was a sexual imbalance between them— the more experienced, unconstrained Hellman and the inhibited Kober, who feared that his wife's pleasure in what he called "going down episodes" was unnatural.[10] And although both were Jews, there was a cultural divide between them: Hellman, who was confidently assimilated, and third-generation, and who could refer to first-generation Eastern Jewish immigrants as "kikes" and "yids," and Kober, who had been born in Poland, one of five children of poor parents who ran a dry goods store in East Harlem, and spoke with an accent which he tried to disguise by affecting English pronunciation.[11] And if Hellman, in her writing, would mention Jews rarely and only in passing, Kober, when he began to write for the *New Yorker*, wrote stories that were almost exclusively about lower-middle-class Jewish characters, their speech rendered in Yiddish cadences, living precisely in the immigrant culture that Hellman disdained.

It was inevitable that as Hellman found her feet she would look for another kind of man. When her friend Lee Gershwin suggested that she be nicer to her sweet husband, she replied that she didn't want a sweet man.[12] She "needed a teacher," she wrote, "a cool teacher, who would not be impressed or disturbed by a strange and difficult girl."[13]

Hellman was difficult, yes, but not particularly strange. No one ever wondered about what Lillian Hellman wanted; she made that evident. When she met Dashiell Hammett she met a man who was truly strange: solitary, unreachable, cold, and inpenetrable in some essential way.

The exact circumstances of the first meeting between Hellman and Hammett have been papered over by many versions. But they met in Hollywood, in a public place, at some sort of party, in the fall of 1930. Hammett was already famous. In legend, at least, Hellman saw Hammett across a crowded room—

tall, handsome, slim, elegantly dressed, soiled from the effects
of a three-day drunk. When she learned his name, she rushed
to his side. According to Hellman, they spent the night in her
car, talking about books.

Neither side of Hammett's family—neither Hammetts nor
Dashiells—bore any resemblance to the Hellmans and Marxes.
Hammett's ancestors were seventeenth-century Catholic set-
tlers from England and France. And through two centuries of
American life, no branch of Hammett's family seems to have
found fortune in America; there is no evidence of accumulated
property or wealth, or of higher education. The Hammetts
and Dashiells stayed pretty much in the class in which they had
begun—farmers, sailors, artisans, clerks, workers.[14] Hammett
was the changeling in the nest.

Hammett was born in 1894, on his grandfather's tobacco
farm in Maryland.[15] Family poverty pushed him into the work-
force at the age of fourteen. But Hammett, a reader since childhood, continued reading after he left school, picking up whatever books came his way, even as he worked odd jobs in the
Baltimore area. In the same way, he picked up the pleasures that
were available to a handsome young boy: smoking, drinking,
sex with prostitutes. These became lifelong habits, of which
he reaped the eventual consequences in alcoholism, frequent
bouts of gonorrhea, and, finally, the emphysema and lung can-
cer that, along with tuberculosis, often made an invalid of him,
and finally killed him at the age of sixty-six.

In 1915, Hammett got a job with the Pinkerton Detective
Agency. His hair was still red in those days. He was tall, intelligent, and probably he already displayed the quality of self-
containment that marked him all his life. He was soon trained
in detective work and sent West to work as a Pinkerton detective. Hammett worked as a Pinkerton until the First World
War broke out when he joined the army. He caught influenza

in the pandemic of 1918, and most of his time in the army was spent in hospitals, being treated for the flu; a latent tuberculosis developed of which he would never be entirely cured.

During a time when he was hospitalized in Tacoma, Hammett met Josephine Dolan, a pretty young nurse. In December 1920, they started dating. In late February of the next year, Hammett was transferred to a hospital in San Diego, and he began writing love letters to the girl he called Jose. Hellman disliked the thought that he had ever loved Jose, but he did:

> This is the first time I ever felt that way about a woman; perhaps it's the first time I have ever really loved a woman. That sounds funny but it may be the truth. . . . Lots of love to the dearest small person in the world. . . . I didn't intend writing you a second letter before I got an answer to my first—but that's the hell of being in love with a vamp. . . . But I love Josephine Anna Dolan and have since the 6th of January, more than anything in Christ's world. . . . Yes'um, I deserve all the love you can spare me and I want a lot more than I deserve.[16]

As he demonstrated during the rest of his life, Hammett was not a marrying man. But he was in love with Jose, and when she became pregnant they married on July 7, 1921. Their daughter, Mary Jane, was born on October 16, 1921. Five years later a second daughter, Josephine, was born.

With little formal education Hammett read unsystematically, but widely. Literature, science, and philosophy. And, almost suddenly it seemed, he began to write. From 1922 through 1934, he published an astonishing body of work—eighty short stories and five novels. Four of his novels appeared between 1929 and 1931. And if Hammett did not actually invent the noir detective story—the hard-boiled, cynical, yet pure-of-heart detective-hero who operated in a bleak, corrupt society—he realized this world so powerfully that his stories and characters entered literature as though a place had been kept for them.

Hammett's biographer, Diane Johnson, sees Hammett's self-portrait in all his detective-heroes: in the fat Continental Op, in Sam Spade, in Elfinstone, the hero of a never-completed novel. Elfinstone, as Hammett wrote him, is "a ruthless man, without manners, impatient of [the] stupidity of people with whom he comes in contact, with little love for his fellows."[17] In particular, Johnson sees Hammett's portrait in Ned Beaumont, the hero of *The Glass Key:* "principled, forlorn, afflicted with an uneasy worldliness and the ability to understand the meaner motives and ambitions of his friends." [18] Johnson adds, "Like Sam Spade, like Nick Charles, Ned will sleep with the woman from a higher social class—pleasure, but also a kind of revenge." In the "Elfinstone" manuscript, Hammett creates a woman who prefigures Hellman—exotic and Jewish: Johnson says that "Hammett liked the idea of Jewish women, and women who were hotblooded and foreign."[19]

In 1929, a year before he met Hellman, Hammett separated from Jose and his children. He would support them—occasionally shower them with money and gifts, more often neglect them for long periods—and never live with them again. That year Hammett went to New York, in part to be where the literary world was centered, but also to join his lover, Nell Martin, to whom he was not quite as exotic a man as he would be to Hellman.[20]

As Hammett had been born into rural poverty, so had Nell Martin, who went into the fields as a berry-picker at the age of ten. She was an adventurous girl, had traveled around the country, taking what work came her way, living the sort of itinerant American life that Woody Guthrie ballads were made of. Martin had driven a taxi, tried law school, worked in laundries, been an actress and a vaudeville singer. And just as unexpectedly as Hammett, she turned out to be a writer.

Martin was not a great writer, or even a particularly good one. Hellman liked to mock her work, but by 1930, when Hellman had written virtually nothing, Nell Martin had published many short stories and some novels and plays. Hammett dedicated his 1930 novel, *The Glass Key*, to her; Martin's 1933 novel, *Lovers Should Marry*, is dedicated to him. Theirs was a not insignificant relationship, and it continued for some time after Hammett and Hellman met.

Dashiell Hammett was not only handsome, rich, and successful when Hellman met him, he was admired for the qualities he gave his heroes— integrity and authenticity. He was seen to be his own man, and he was, but authenticity is a quality that can belong to both the devil and the saint.

Everybody drank a lot in those days. Hammett drank ruinously. If Hellman liked to see him as a "stylish" drunk, others would differ. He could be a falling-in-the-gutter drunk, a three-day-binge drunk, a vomiting drunk, a drunk who couldn't remember what he had done when drunk. Often he was a violent drunk. Hellman was sometimes seen with bruises on her face. Once, at a party Hammett punched her in the jaw so hard that she fell to the floor.[21] An actress named Elise De Viane successfully sued Hammett for assault and battery.[22] Hammett could be a cruel drunk; he was certainly cruel when he called across the dinner table to an actress, no longer very young, who had just spilled tomato sauce on her lap: "Doesn't it remind you of when we were both still menstruating?"[23] "Oh, Pru," he said of one of his lovers, "She just thinks you can't fuck her without paying attention to her. So I . . . did a crossword over her shoulder while I screwed her."[24]

Hammett never gave up prostitutes, or other women, for that matter. He sometimes wanted Hellman to take part in sexual threesomes; and Hellman, in love with him, drinking and smoking heavily to keep up with him, trying to keep up with him in every way, did what she could to please him.[25] It was the

1930s, the Depression had hit the country, but for Hellman and Hammett Fitzgerald's Jazz Age seemed to linger.

> There was the odor of tobacco always—both of them smoked incessantly; it was in their clothes, their blankets, the curtains, and the ash-littered carpets. Added to this was the wretched aura of stale wine, with its inevitable suggestion of beauty gone foul and revelry remembered in disgust.[26]

There is no need to ask what kept Hellman with Hammett: Sexual excitement, Hammett's good looks, his fame as a writer, his natural air of authority, the thrilling, transgressive edge he offered of life without boundaries, the politics she soon came to share with him. And when he went on the wagon he showed her the life of a writer deeply concentrated on work; then he was the "cool teacher" she wanted, generous to Hellman with his intellectual life, with his ideas about writing; generous also with his money, which in those days poured in like Monopoly money, and which was hers as much as his.

Yet four months after meeting Hammett, Hellman decamped for New York, leaving Hammett, and also Arthur Kober, who was still very much part of her life. Hammett was caught by surprise, which may have been the point. Kober was distraught but not yet despairing. Jose came to see Kober one day, wanting to know how serious the Hammett-Hellman relationship was. She still hoped Hammett would come back to her and the children. Kober told Jose not to worry. It was just a passing fling.

If Kober believed this, it was because Hellman gave him reason. From New York she wrote to her husband, begging him to "please love me." She told him that "I miss you an awful lot. . . . I love you very much. . . . Certainly I'm coming back & if you want me sooner I'll leave right away. . . . I hope we are going to stay married the rest of our lives."[27] And, "I dreamed about you last night. . . . I think about you too much. I'm a thinker type."[28] She spoke about having children with him.

Hellman was keeping her options open. She was writing to Hammett, too. He did not keep her letters, but she kept his. Hammett wrote teasingly, offering himself in one sentence, withdrawing in the next; speaking of love, and mocking it: "The emptiness I thought was hunger for chow mein turned out to be for you, so maybe a cup of beef tea. . . . So you're not coming home, eh? I suppose it doesn't make any difference if I have to go on practically masturbating . . ."[29]

Really, Kober never had a chance. He and Hellman divorced early in 1932, after eight years of marriage. Hellman's tortuous years with Hammett began. Her life as a writer began.

5

———◆·◆·◆———

The Writing Life: 1933–1984

"My ambition now is to collect enough money to be able to finish 'The Thin Man,' which God willing, will be my last detective novel . . ." So Hammett wrote to Hellman in 1931.[1]

The Thin Man was published in 1934. Hammett was forty, prime time for a writer, but *The Thin Man* would be his last novel in any genre, and his literary silence persisted for the twenty-odd years of life left to him. He had not lost the ambition to write; on the contrary. Through the years he would refer, optimistically or despairingly, to a book he was working on, whether the same book or several, is not clear.[2] All that was found at his death was a fragment of a novel which he called "Tulip." Hellman would publish this, together with some of his early stories, and her introduction to them, in a collection called *The Big Knockover*.

Hammett's alcoholism, his bouts of ill health—recurrences of gonorrhea, eruptions of tuberculosis, periods of depression—

all these surely weakened and demoralized him, and ate into his time and energy. But his silence descended so quickly after *The Thin Man;* no sooner did he announce his ambition to abandon the detective genre, than he seems to have hit the wall that every writer fears is looming—when he has written himself out, exhausted his material, run out his string. Hammett was a constant and discerning reader; he understood good writing. His contemporaries, his friends, included William Faulkner, Scott Fitzgerald, and Ernest Hemingway. Hammett was popular and admired, but it was the others, not he, who set the literary standards for the time.

At the end of 1948, Hammett went on the wagon for good, but it made no difference to his ability to write, and painfully, and over many years, he must have discovered that his talent would not stretch to reach his literary ambition. He couldn't go back to detective stories, he felt he had worn that vein of his writing out; and he couldn't find his way ahead. This was Hammett's tragedy, the tragedy of a writing life.

Nothing similar would blight Hellman's life. She had failures, yes, and she suffered over them. But she had a sense of what she could do, and when she failed, she got over it, and wrote again.

In a desultory way, Hellman had been writing since the 1920s. Arthur Kober had published some of Hellman's stories in *The Paris Comet.* In 1933 and in early 1934 Hellman published two stories in the *American Spectator,* slight, humorous *New Yorker*ish stories (though they had been rejected by the *New Yorker*) more in Kober's broad style than the tightly constructed melodramatic style for which Hellman became known. In the early thirties Hellman also collaborated with her former lover, Louis Kronenberger, on a never-to-be produced farce, which they called *The Dear Queen.*

Life is full of "what-ifs," and would Hellman have become a playwright if she had not cast her lot with Hammett's? Certainly she would not have written *The Children's Hour*. In 1933, as Hammett was finishing up *The Thin Man*, he came across a recounting by William Roughead of a legal case—"Closed Doors; or, The Great Drumsheugh Case": In early nineteenth-century Scotland, two young school teachers were accused by an unhappy pupil of harboring an "unnatural" affection for each other. The teachers went to court to deny the accusation; they won their case, but their school and their lives were ruined. Hammett toyed with the idea of making a play of this material himself, but he offered it to Hellman, and it became *The Children's Hour*.

Hellman stuck with the essentials of the story, changing emphases here and there. Her main task was to learn the craft of playwrighting, how to transform a story into dialogue that played on the stage. Hammett worked with her on draft after draft. The couple moved around a lot during 1933 and 1934. Sometimes they were together, sometimes apart. They stayed at various hotels in New York, they spent time in the Florida Keys, on a Connecticut island, on Long Island. Wherever Hellman happened to be that year, she worked steadily on *The Children's Hour*. With Hammett's guidance she produced at least six drafts of the script. It was not finished until he gave it his imprimatur. She was grateful to him, and she resented him; she depended on him for encouragement, for ruthless editing, for rewriting until he died. After that, perhaps coincidentally, she never again wrote an original play.

Like every writer, Hellman was often in despair about her work. She was a complainer by nature, and perhaps she complained more than most. In 1944, when Hellman had three hits—*The Children's Hour*, *The Little Foxes*, and *Watch on the Rhine*—behind her, as well as one failure, *Days to Come*, she was working on her fifth play, *The Searching Wind*. Hammett was unavailable to her. He was in the army, stationed in the Aleutians. She wrote him a letter complaining of how badly her work was going. He answered: "If you had any memory . . . you'd know that your present dithers over the play are only the normal bellyaching of La Hellman at work. You still think you dashed those other plays off without a fear, a groan or a sigh; but you didn't sister: I haven't had a dry shoulder since your career began."[3] In another letter from the Aleutians, Hammett affectionately, teasingly, evoked the atmosphere of their work together: "Oh yes," he wrote, "about you: I hope the play is coming along better than if I was on hand to get into quarrels with you about it, and that therefor[e] you are devoting to sheer writing those periods you used to take out for sulking because I was hampering your art or objecting to a glittering generality, which, it's possible, is the same thing."[4]

Hellman had a finished script of *The Children's Hour* in 1934. She gave it to Herman Shumlin, the director and producer who had made his name on Broadway with the production of *Grand Hotel*. It was not a blind submission. Hellman knew Shumlin; she worked for him, sporadically, as a script reader. Shumlin agreed to produce the play, and it opened in November of 1934, a major first play, and a major hit. The reviews were spectacular: "the season's dramatic high-water mark," from the *New Yorker* critic. The material—lesbianism—was scandalous (the play was banned in Boston). *The Children's Hour* ran on Broadway for more than two years, and when the Pulitzer Prize Committee gave the prize to an adaptation of an Edith Wharton story, *The Old Maid*, the New York drama critics created the Drama Critics' Circle Awards, and gave one to Hellman. She was twenty-nine and famous. In the middle of the Depression, Sam Goldwyn offered her $2,500 a week to write screenplays; she was rich. She had more lovers than she could easily juggle: Herman Shumlin would soon be her lover, also the editor and publisher, Ralph Ingersoll, Hammett, of course, the producer and director Jed Harris, Arthur Kober from time to time, and others as the fancy took her.

Failure came to Hellman with her second play. In 1935, still riding high on the success of *The Children's' Hour*, Hellman began work on *Days to Come*. This time she supplied her own plot, which announced her political interests. *Days to Come* centers on relations between labor and capital in the form of a strike in a one-industry Ohio town. A union organizer arrives in town: a very attractive man, a man of integrity, perhaps not unlike Hammett. The villains are strike-breakers, hired by the mill owner who, in ordinary times, is a decent enough man, kind and paternalistic to his employees. But in this time of crisis he shows his true colors as a capitalist by hiring thugs to break the strike.

But the issues of the strike are confused. The characters are little more than stick figures with attitudes, and the social problems that Hellman wants us to care about don't seem to interest her very much. Her attention is on the secondary plot: on the unhappy, adulterous wife of the mill owner who falls in love with the union organizer. Love is doomed. In the end everyone speaks truth to everyone else and everyone's life is changed, if not necessarily for the better.

The critics noticed that Hellman did not have a grip on her play. When *Days to Come* opened in mid-December 1936, William Randolph Hearst walked out during the second act, and much of the audience with him. The reviews were devastating. The *New York Post* reviewer called it "dull" and "muddled," the *New York Times* found it not only "bitter" and "elusive" with an "analysis of female neuroticism" thrown in. The play closed after six performances.

Hellman feared for her career. "The truth is I'm scared of plotting, that the few things I've ever done well were plots laid out for me beforehand," she wrote to Arthur Kober.[5] She was referring to the screenplays she had adapted from material originating with other writers; and, of course, she was speaking of Dashiell Hammett, her greatest literary resource, who had given her the plot for *The Children's Hour.* Hammett had not been of much use to her on *Days to Come.* For long periods in 1936 he was enduring treatments for gonorrhea, and drinking very heavily. When he saw the play on opening night, he didn't like it, and he told her so.

Failure threw Hellman off balance, but only temporarily. In the late winter of 1937, she and Hammett went to Hollywood; Hellman to adapt Sidney Kingsley's Broadway hit, *Dead End* for the screen, Hammett to work on a third *Thin Man* script. They lived together in apparent harmony, in a six-bedroom suite at the Beverly Wilshire Hotel. Both worked to organize the Screen Writers Guild, to assure that Hollywood writers got proper credit for their work. In late spring or early summer Hellman became pregnant. In her memoirs she says that for a little while she imagined the possibility of marriage and a normal family life with Hammett, and that he, too, seemed pleased about the prospect. He went so far as to get a Mexican divorce from Jose, which may or may not have had legal force. But just as talk of marriage was in the air, Hammett went on a drunken binge and brought a woman home to their bed. Hellman had an abortion. (Her seventh, according to her friend Lee Gershwin.)[6] In late August, after *Dead End* had been released to excellent reviews, Hellman sailed for France on the *Normandie.* She returned from her travels in November and began work on her third play, *The Little Foxes*, which turned out to be her second huge success. *The Children's Hour* had not been a fluke.

As Hellman later realized when she, herself, was teaching, writing for the theater was something that couldn't be taught: "Playwriting," she told an interviewer, "is something you have to come by instinctively, be born to."[7] She also understood that writing was not a matter of mood but required regular working hours. She worked three hours in the morning, two or three hours in the afternoon, another two or three hours late in the evening.[8]

As for the process, Hellman echoed the bemusement of many writers: "How the pages got there, in their form, in their order is more of a mystery than reason would hope for," she wrote.[9] She called *The Little Foxes* "the most difficult play I ever wrote," and of all her plays, she said, she had depended on Hammett most heavily for this one.[10] "I was clumsy in the first drafts, putting in and taking out characters, ornamenting, decorating, growing more and more weary as the versions of scenes and then acts and then whole plays had to be thrown away. I was on the eighth version of the play before Hammett gave a nod of approval and said he thought everything would be O.K. if only I'd cut out the 'blackamoor chit chat.'" It wasn't easy for her to endure "the toughness of his criticism, the coldness of his praise," but it was useful to her "and I knew it."[11]

The writing of *Watch on the Rhine* was a comparative pleasure: "the only play I have ever written that came out in one piece, as if I had seen a landscape and never altered the trees or the seasons of their colors. All other work for me had been fragmented, hunting in an open field . . . following the course but unable to see clearly . . . But here, for the first and last time, the work I did . . . make[s] a pleasant oneness. . ."[12]

Perhaps Hellman's sense of wholeness in the play was due to the unity of her theme. *The Little Foxes* of 1939 had also had a theme: the indictment of greed and, implicitly, the injustices of capitalism. But in that play the relationships between the Hubbards were so discordant, that although rivalry for riches was the subject, attention was deflected from the theme to the family members. In *Watch on the Rhine*, plot and characters work smoothly to serve the story. There are many dramatic twists and turns in the plot of *Rhine*, including her hero's act of

murder, but everything that happens is directly to the point—
Fascism, Nazism, is an evil that must be fought; and not only
by the Europeans who have experienced the Nazi rise to power,
but by complacent American liberals as well. *Watch on the Rhine*
is an exhortation to America to face the facts of the European
war, and to act. It was produced in April 1941, eight months
before Pearl Harbor, after which that matter was resolved.

In 1939 Hellman had been asked by an interviewer whether
she thought literature should have social or economic implications. "No, I don't," she said first; then she contradicted herself: "I do feel that all good writing must, either implicitly, or
explicitly, be propaganda for something . . . unless you are a
pathological escapist there must be some sort of propaganda
in everything you write." But Hellman saw the danger in the
word "propaganda"; she did not want to be thought of as a
writer with a political agenda. She fumbled for a bit over the
definition of the word, and decided to equate it with truth: So,
"Some sort of truth . . ." she said, "truth must be the main ob-
jective of anyone who seeks a form of literary expression . . . If
a person doesn't want to involve himself with the truth he has
no business trying to write at all."[13]

Hellman was a prolific writer, and when she stopped producing plays after almost thirty years she was naturally asked why.
She had a variety of explanations: she said that she was tired of
the theater, that it had never been her natural home, that people
in the theater spoke of nothing but money. But it was also true
she had begun in the theater with Hammett at her side, and
she abandoned the theater when he left her. Her final play, an
adaptation of a novel *My Mother, My Father and Me*, was produced a year after Hammett's death and was a resounding flop.

In the mid-1960s an article in the drama section of the
New York Times named Arthur Miller, Tennessee Williams, and

Edward Albee as the three major living American playwrights. Hellman had a fit. To Peter Feibleman, who was staying with her at her Martha's Vineyard house, she said: "There are people who can stand to be forgotten and people who can't." In Feibleman's telling it was on that very morning that Hellman made the decision to write a memoir.[14]

An Unfinished Woman was published in 1969. The book went to the top of the best-seller list and won a National Book Award. Some reviewers noticed that Hellman was evasive about her personal and public life, but saw her reserve as a sign of personal strength: "Most readers," Stanley Young wrote in the *New York Times Book Review*, "will respond to her book because it not only shows rare imagination and literary skill but reveals with an almost sad reluctance the unexpected personal story of a great American playwright."

Hellman's reputation soared, and she continued writing memoirs—*Pentimento, Scoundrel Time, Maybe*—until the very end of her life. In 1984, the year she died, when she was blind and could not breathe without supplemental oxygen, Hellman collaborated with Feibleman, her late-life companion, to write *Eating Together*, a compilation of recipes and meals they had cooked and shared. She just missed seeing its publication.

6

Along Came a Spider

WHEN HELLMAN took off for Europe in August 1937, she
was in the company of her good friend Dorothy Parker, and
Parker's husband, Alan Campbell. By chance, Martha Gellhorn
was also on board. Gellhorn was then at the beginning of her
affair with Ernest Hemingway, and was on her way to spend
several days with him in Paris before traveling with him to the
war in Spain.

After several weeks of a purely social time with Parker and
Campbell in Paris, Hellman entrained for Moscow, where she
had been invited to attend a theater festival. Whether she did,
or did not, break her journey in Berlin to give her friend Julia
money for the anti-Nazi underground would become a matter of dispute in Hellman's later years. Nevertheless, she was
certainly in Moscow in 1937, where she saw a number of plays
that she says she did not much enjoy. Naturally, she spoke with
the English-speaking people she met in Moscow, most of them

diplomats, foreign journalists, and other invited visitors. In later years Hellman puzzled over her ignorance of events then occurring in Moscow: "I did not even know," she wrote, "I was there in the middle of the ugliest purge period, and I have often asked myself how that could be."[1]

This is a good question; and although Hellman raises it herself, she lets it dangle, unanswered. In 1979, when the three volumes of her memoirs were published under one cover, Hellman elaborated on her ignorance, implying that not only she, but Hammett, too, had been unaware of the purges until she, herself, brought him the news: "Later, when I knew about the purges, I bought a history of the Moscow trials and Hammett and I read aloud from it, saying things like 'lawyers are lawyers wherever their training,' and about Vishinsky, the prosecuting attorney, 'what a tricky old bastard.'"[2]

When Hellman wrote those words, Hammett was dead and unable to confirm his disdain of the legal profession. But that aside, since Hellman twice insists on her ignorance of the purges, it seems fair to press her on the matter. How *could* it have been that she knew nothing of them?

"In the West the facts were readily available. Hundreds of articles and books were published," Robert Conquest wrote in *The Great Terror*, his definitive book on the purges.[3] By the time Hellman got to Moscow in late September 1937, two of the three public trials had already been held. The names of the defendants were well known to anyone with the least interest in the Bolshevik revolution. The defendants were, in fact, a large part of the founding leadership of the Soviet Union, the Old Bolsheviks who had stood with Lenin and Trotsky in October 1917. Now, twenty years later, they were on trial as traitors. One after another they confessed to the most incredible plots against Stalin and the Soviet Union. Invariably these plots involved them in conspiracies with Leon Trotsky, denounced as an agent of the Nazis, and various other capitalist governments. "These mad dogs of capitalism," as the prosecutor, Andrei Vishinksy, described the defendants, were bent on assassinating Stalin and tearing the Soviet Union "limb from limb."[4]

When warned that the purges might turn sympathetic opinion in the West against him, Stalin knew better: "Never mind," he said. "They'll swallow it."[5]

Walter Duranty was one of the journalists with whom Hellman spoke in Moscow. He was bureau chief for the *New York Times*, and well-known as an "unofficial spokesman for the Kremlin."[6] In the early 1930s Duranty had denied what was clearly true—the existence of a deliberately created famine in the Ukraine in which millions died of starvation. In 1936, after the first purge trial, he wrote: "It is inconceivable that a public trial of such men would be held unless the authorities had full proofs of their guilt." In January 1937, after the second trial, Duranty lamented the lack of any documentary evidence of the defendants' guilt, but he thought that taken all in all the trial did stand up.

In the same paragraph of an *Unfinished Woman*, in which Hellman wonders about her ignorance of the purges, she writes, "I saw a number of diplomats and journalists [in Moscow] but they talked such gobbledygook [about the purges] with the exception of Walter Duranty."

It would not be a leap from this sentence to infer that Hellman already knew what Duranty had written, and that he confirmed her already formed opinion. In any case, the trials had caused a great deal of consternation and discussion in Hellman's circles; she could not have escaped being aware of them. Her claim to have come to Moscow in ignorance is clumsily made, and simply unbelievable. Why did she bother to deny knowing what the whole world knew? Knowing what every Communist knew and believed: "We cannot claim we did not know what was happening," Peggy Dennis, wife of the post-war General Secretary of the American Communist Party wrote. "We read of the public trials. . . . We saw it as part of the brutal realities of making revolution, of building an oasis of socialism in a sea of enemies. We accepted the belief of infallibility of our leaders, the wisdom of our Party."[7]

By the time Hellman returned home from her adventures in Europe, she evidently felt well-enough informed about the purges to take a public position. Along with Dashiell Hammett and other luminaries, she signed a petition headed: "Leading Artists, Educators Support Soviet Trial Verdict." The signers accused the Soviet defendants of "duplicity and conspiracy," of having "allied themselves with long standing enemies of the Soviet Union . . . even with former czarist *agents provocateurs.*"

The petition used the brutal language that did not come naturally to the American signers, but was in common usage in Soviet Russia: "Degeneration . . . eradication of spies and wreckers."[8]

Two years later, in 1939, in an "Open Letter to American Liberals," Hellman and Hammett would warn their countrymen of the danger of offering Leon Trotsky asylum in the United States, "which would give support to fascist forces."[9] The timing was unfortunate; only a week later the Nazi-Soviet Pact was signed, and Communists and their sympathizers all over the world decided that fascism was not really so bad after all, simply a matter of taste. Except for Trotsky, in whose case it was still a criminal activity. The death sentence imposed on him in absentia in Moscow was carried out in 1940 in his Mexican exile.

But before she returned to the United States in 1937, and some weeks after leaving Moscow, Hellman was back in Paris. There, one night, she had dinner with Otto Katz. Hellman knew Katz as "a Communist who, the year I met him, was a kind of press chief for the Spanish Republican Government. . . . he persuaded me that I must go to Spain. It didn't take much persuasion; I had strong convictions about the Spanish war, about Fascism-Nazism, strong enough to push just below the surface my fear of the danger of war."[10]

Katz, who went by many names, including André Simone, Otto Simon, and Rudolph Breda, was well known as "a propagandist of genius."[11] He was, by all accounts a charming man, a ladies' man, attractive, and an "unconscionable flatter," according to Arthur Koestler, who knew him well. He may well have been Hellman's lover. She admired him so highly that she took Katz as her model for the heroic character of Kurt Muller in her play, *Watch on the Rhine*.[12] Like so many other loyal Communists who spent their lives in aid of the cause, Katz would later pay with his life when he was convicted and hanged for treason in the Czechoslovakian show trial of 1952. Meanwhile, in 1937, he urged Hellman to go to Spain.

Many writers had congregated in Spain to bear witness and to write about the Spanish Civil War. Hemingway was in Spain with Martha Gellhorn, as was Josephine Herbst and John Dos Passos. Dorothy Parker and her husband Alan Campbell were there, quite possibly traveling with Hellman.

A reader of Hellman's memoirs would infer that she had endured the dangers of wartime Spain on her own. But a letter in Hellman's FBI files suggests otherwise. Steve Nelson, a prominent leader of the American Communist Party, and for many years a Comintern agent, wrote to Hellman in August 1943, reminding her of their meeting in Spain: "Anyway we met in Valencia in 1937 with Dorothy Parker, Allen [sic] Campbell, Lasser and Louis Fischer."[13]

For Hellman the issues of the Spanish Civil War were simple—a democratically elected government, supported only by the Soviet Union, was fighting for its existence against a Fascist coup supported by Hitler and Mussolini.

For others on the Left, on close inspection the issues became more complicated. George Orwell noticed that the Soviets had their own agenda in Spain; he wrote about Soviet intrigues and motives in his classic book on the war, *Homage to Catalonia* (which, as late as the 1970s, Hellman called "a load of crap").[14] John Dos Passos noticed problems in Spain when he searched for his Spanish friend, Jose Robles, and learned that Robles had been killed by the Soviets. "Fascists and communists alike shot the best men first," Dos Passos wrote.[15] As even the novelist and journalist Josephine Herbst, for all her sympathy with the Soviet Union, acknowledged when, in April 1938, she wrote to her friend Katherine Anne Porter: "What I know is that Russia should not have let Spain down, not for anything."[16]

In Spain as in Moscow, Hellman heard what she wanted to hear: "[A] great many people have told me a great many things . . . [about] nuns and priests torn by the limbs in Republican villages . . . why what government fell when; the fights among the Anarchists and Communists and Socialists; who is on one side today who wasn't yesterday—but this is not the way I learn things and so I have only half-listened."[17]

If Hellman did not learn by reading, if she dismissed views that contradicted her own as "gobbledygook," how then *did* she learn? Perhaps we can say that she did not learn, she simply *knew:* she *knew* that she was, as Tony Judt once wrote of the Communists of her generation, that she was part of "an idea and a movement uncompromisingly attached to representing and defending the interests of the wretched of the earth."[18] Not only was Communism a powerful idea, it could be reduced to slogans. "One of the causes of the popularity of Marxism among educated people was the fact that in its simple form it was very easy," the Polish philosopher Leszek Kołakowski, wrote. "It is an instrument that made it possible to master all of history and economics, without actually having to study either." The Marxist system "simply solves all of the problems of mankind at one stroke."[19]

And indeed, Hellman was not much interested in mustering arguments for her ideas. Her response to opposition was usually anger. Stopping in London on her way from Spain to New York, Hellman went to a dinner party at the home of an old friend who announced to the table that Lillian had just returned from the war in Spain: "Which side did you choose to visit, Miss Hellman?" a guest asked her. "Each has an argument I dare say."

"I suddenly was in the kind of rampage anger that I have known all my life, still know, and certainly in those days was not able, perhaps did not wish, to control. I left the table so fast that I turned over my chair, left the house so fast that I forgot my coat and was not cold on a winter night, threw myself down so hard on the hotel bed that I slipped to the floor, had a painful ankle and didn't care."[20]

Arthur Kober, to whom Hellman remained close all his life, kept track of her political progress in his diary: "Lil, who has just found the cause, speaks like expert & like all those eloquent dogmatists will not allow anyone else to think or listen to what is being said."[21] On May 6, 1935, Kober noted, "Lil talks revolution."[22] Soon after Hellman's return from her visit to the Soviet Union and Spain, Kober noted that in Hellman's opinion Russia was "the ideal democratic state."[23]

Political analysis was not Hellman's strong suit; her mind was most comfortably at home with the absolute. Still, in the late 1960s, when she was beginning to work on her memoirs, she might have acknowledged the guiding idea to which she had held fast for so many years. Instead she brushed it away: "I could have answered some of those charges [of Stalinism] a long time ago," Hellman wrote, "but it was a complex story and didn't seem worth the try. And, like most people I don't like explaining myself when I am under attack. . . . The truth is that I never thought about Stalin at all."[24]

Not exactly so. But nothing in Hellman's nature would have permitted her to admit that she was not an independent

thinker. She also had, as the critic Clive James noted, "pro-
nounced tendencies towards that brand of aggressive humility,
or claimed innocence, which finds itself helpless to explain the
world at the very moment when the reader is well justified in
requiring that a writer should give an apprehensible outline of
what he deems to be going on."[25]

The numbers of those faithful to the Communist idea diminished with the years until Hellman stood virtually alone. In
1967 the lid of the Pandora's Box where she kept her politics
cracked open for a moment. On an evening of that year, while
visiting Blair Clark, her love interest of the moment, Hellman said to him, "I can't get it out of my head that Stalin was
right."[26]

7

◆─◆─◆

Eros

On April 24, 1967, Lillian Hellman made an entry in her diary. She was traveling in France with a man she calls "R" and she reflected on the nature of their relations: "The years we have known each other have made a pleasant summer fog of the strange, crippled relationship, often ripped, always mended, merging finally into comfort." A moment later, as she and "R" are sipping liqueurs and chatting pleasantly in the garden of their hotel, "R" rips the relationship once again. He begins with an ominous sentence: "I must say something to you." And what he says is that he has fallen passionately in love with a young woman, and feels that he "should get married again." He throws Hellman a sop: "My feeling for you has kept me from marrying."[1]

Hellman was sixty-two years old at the time of this incident. "R," whom she does not identify in her memoirs, was fifty, and his name was Blair Clark; he was handsome, rich, and socially prominent.[2] During the five or six years of their distinctly strange half-love affair, half exercise in sadomasochism, which Hellman chronicled in her diaries, she has courted him assiduously. "I love you very much," she wrote to him, "and I miss you so hard that I can see you come in the door."[3] For his part, Clark has broken her heart numberless times in affairs with many other women, and has never once consented to go to bed with her, excusing himself on the grounds that sex would spoil the special nature of their friendship.

Hellman seemed to take that excuse at its face value, and to believe that in time she could change Clark's mind. The situation is heartbreaking, awesome, and inexplicable: heartbreaking in the depth and desperation of Hellman's need; awesome in her determination to prevail; and inexplicable in that for all her worldly experience, Hellman could not fathom that the laws of the sexual marketplace applied to her.

By the time she reached middle-age, Hellman's sexual history was densely populated. She had begun fairly early for her time, at nineteen. Of her first sexual experience, she wrote, "The few months it lasted did not mean much to me, but I have often asked myself whether I underestimated the damage that so loveless an arrangement made on my future. But my generation did not often deal with the idea of love . . . And we were suspicious of the words of love."[4] Her suspicion extended to the words that imply love: monogamy, fidelity, betrayal. On a visit to Moscow in 1944, she wrote that she found the Russians "romantic and dawn-fogged about sex" and their "talk about love and fidelity too high-minded for my history or my taste."[5]

As she had begun, so she continued. In principle at least, Hellman believed that sex meant neither more or less than you wanted it to mean: it might be an act of love, or a physical pleasure that could be taken with anyone, without consequence. Hammett had acted on this idea consistently, and Hellman gave almost as good as she got. But to do so, she had to fight a nature that had always been tormented by jealousy: "I made a sound I had never heard myself make before," Hellman writes of the feeling of jealousy that overcame her in early adolescence. Sexually stirred by "Willy" (her uncle by marriage), she had watched him go off with his Cajun girlfriend: "I believe that what I felt that night was what I was to feel" as a grown woman, the "humiliation of vanity . . . rejection . . . I was at one minute less than nothing and, at another, powerful enough to revenge myself with the murder of Willy."[6]

Adding fuel to jealousy was Hellman's bitter awareness that she was not a beauty; that in a room of beautiful women she would not, in the normal course of things, be the one preferred. But as far as she could manage it, neither would she allow herself to be chosen against. Whether by willed decision or natural assertiveness, from her youth to middle-age, few beautiful women could equal Hellman's sexual success; few had her boldness, her presence, her nerve.

To begin with, as Hellman once noted, youth, alone, is a powerful aphrodisiac: "All the men in the [Liveright] office made routine passes at the girls who worked there—one would have had to be hunchbacked to be an exception."[7] And after the success of *The Children's Hour*, Hellman was in possession of a double dose of attraction: she was still young, and now she had fame as well. She would retain the power of fame all her life, and what she had going for her outlasted youth: immense vitality, intelligence, a sharp wit, a good figure. And even more: an urgent need for the attentions of men, a lack of inhibition in making her desires known, a strong sex drive, and the wish to please. Apparently, no lover was ever disappointed. "Unbelievably seductive," said one lover. Another man, who did not initially find her attractive, let himself be seduced, and once in bed with her found the experience "just unbelievable . . . anything went . . . anything . . . it was terrific."[8] Yet another lover,

James Roosevelt, the President's son, called her "the greatest lay I ever had."[9] Not every man fell in love with her, but many did, attractive, successful men, the publisher Ralph Ingersoll, for one, who often promised to leave his wife for her, although he never did.

In the early 1940s, more than a decade after their beginning, Hellman and Hammett's sex life came to an end.[10] As they were driving to a party, Hammett put his hand on Hellman's knee and suggested they skip the event, go home, make a pitcher of martinis, and take it to bed. For whatever reason—the lure of a glamorous party, an unattractively drunk Hammett—Hellman said no. And for whatever reason, Hammett decided to take Hellman's refusal as final. They never made love again.[11] Or it may be that it was Hellman who decided. She told the story both ways.[12]

By this time, each had had many other sexual partners; inevitably their sexual bond had weakened and resentments had mounted. Hellman hated Hammett's bouts of incapacitating and violent drunkenness; his coldness which kept her at a distance; his silence in the face of her rebukes; his parade of women, whether prostitutes or, sometimes, friends, as when Hammett, to Hellman's lifelong fury, spent a week with their mutual friend, Laura Perelman, wife of S. J. Perelman, and sister of Nathanael West; with whom, as it had happened, Hellman had had her own brief affair.

Hammett's habit was silence and evasion, but he had his own resentments: of Hellman's frequent rages, of her refusal to accept the fact that he was a man who would not tolerate interference with his life, of her social ambitions, which irritated him. And when Hammett began to understand that he would not write again, he would have had to be more than human not to feel some bitterness at this essential loss, particularly when measured against Hellman's growing success, given that they both knew how much she owed it to him.

In the spring of 1939, with the success of *The Little Foxes*, Hellman bought a 130-acre estate in Westchester County. She turned it into a working farm, Hardscrabble Farm she called it, which she and Hammett worked together. The farm was in Hellman's name, but Hammett contributed to the expense of running it. He loved the place, and came and went as he pleased. As they lived separately in the city, they had separate bedrooms and lives at the farm. Hellman's friends and lovers often trooped up to the farm on weekends, and she was open about her affairs—with her producer, Herman Shumlin, with St. Clair McKelway the *New Yorker* writer, with *Time* writer Charles Wertenbaker, with any number of other men. She preferred tall, handsome men, Lillian's "goys," Arthur Kober called them.[13] Some affairs were serious—the one with Shumlin lasted some years—others were brief, not always by Hellman's choice.

For all the frenetic sexual activity, deep, reciprocal love eluded Hellman. No one was writing the sort of poems to her that her poet friend Theodore Roethke wrote to his wife: "I knew a woman, lovely in her bones." Did she want that? More and more as time went on.

In Moscow, at the end of 1944, Hellman met a diplomat named John Melby. Melby was no poet but he was an intelligent, capable man, and he was enraptured by Hellman. He fell deeply in love with her, he felt sexually awakened. She had "made a man" of him, he said; she "knew how to make a man feel like a man."[14] When Melby left his posting in Moscow in 1945, he and Hellman spent the summer together at Hardscrabble Farm and at East Hampton. Hellman introduced him to her friends, including Hammett, and including her psychoanalyst, Gregory Zilboorg, who evidently approved of Melby

as a lover for Hellman. When Melby left for his new posting
to China, Zilboorg wrote to him encouraging the relationship:
he believed that Melby and Lillian "were happy together and
would be."[15]

When Melby went to China, Hellman briefly considered
going with him. She did not go. It was inconceivable that she
would give up her life to be hostess for a diplomat. But she
and Melby wrote each other frequently and at length. Melby
invested in *Another Part of the Forest*, which opened in late 1946.
He sent Hellman expensive hand-woven silk from Nanking.
He reminded her of their happy times and spoke of his hopes
that they would be together again.

But they were an odd couple. Time and distance worked
against them, and so did their political differences. Melby was a
colleague of George Kennan, and shared Kennan's understanding of the Soviet regime. He held no brief for Stalin's policies,
or, for that matter, for those of the American Communist Party.
Henry Wallace, whose Progressive Party bid for the presidency
in 1948, was actively supported by the American Communist
Party, and by Hellman, raised Melby's ire. In November 1947,
he wrote to Hellman: "I . . . think it most unseemly of Wallace to make the kind of speech he does abroad [attacking the
Marshall Plan]. If he disagrees let him do it at home." In another letter, he wrote, "I do in fact think you are wrong about
events and about a lot of people . . . it is plain now that the
United States is faced with expanding Slavic power which is
without scruples of any kind." In answer to a letter from Hellman which does not survive, Melby wrote, "Of course I realize
what all this [disagreement] implies of a personal nature, and
that is the hardest part. On the other hand, I see nothing to be
gained, and much to be lost by pretending one is what one is
not."[16] In February 1948, with the Wallace campaign in high
gear, Melby wrote: "I'm sorry to say I think Wallace is making
a damned fool of himself. . . . Isn't the record clear enough by

now that [the Communists] will simply use him for their own ends . . . [and] that those ends are bad? . . . simply an extension of Soviet power, and they will never hesitate to use any means available to secure that extension . . . I don't quite see what it has to do with Jeffersonian democracy."[17]

The love affair was essentially over by 1948, although affection remained and Hellman and Melby continued to see each other on occasion. In the early 1950s, when McCarthyism was at its height, Melby's loyalty was questioned. The State Department's Loyalty Security Board offered only one charge against him: "That during the period 1945 to date, you have maintained an association with one Lillian Hellman, reliably reported to be a member of the Communist Party." Melby was fired from the State Department in 1953. Unable to get a job in government, he taught for a while at a Canadian university. His name was finally cleared in 1980.[18]

In the late forties, with Melby in China and their love affair fading, Hellman looked elsewhere. A casual affair with Randall Smith, an ex-longshoreman and veteran of the Spanish Civil War, filled some time. In 1948, a more serious prospect appeared. She began an affair with the Deputy Foreign Minister of Yugoslavia, Srdja Prica. Of Prica, Hellman wrote in her diary: "I am probably doing it all over again—but someday soon the need must be fulfilled—it is getting late."[19] She suspected the affair would not turn out well. Prica was a "sharp handsome and aggressive," man, a famous womanizer.[20] He was a very unlikely prospect to fulfill the need Hellman felt for a constant lover, for a husband, possibly even for a child, although she was by then in her early forties. For a little while, before Prica dropped her, she hoped against hope that "His Excellency," as she later referred to him, would be that man.

Hellman lived a daring sexual life; as with all daring enterprises it had dangers: for one thing she exposed herself to that most common and painful danger, rejection. Sexual rejection cut particularly deeply with Hellman who felt her lack of beauty, and diminishing youth. But she did not change her seductive technique. "Lillian came on with every man she met," Arthur Miller said. Miller wasn't interested, and he felt that she never forgave him for that. Nor was the director Elia Kazan interested. Hellman invited him to a dinner à deux. In his memoirs Kazan writes of the evening: "I felt like a young girl cornered by a rich old man who expected the reward she could afford to pay for the fine meal he was providing." Kazan might not have been unwilling but: "I saw that her general attitude toward the world was derisive. She made fun of everyone she talked about, and I wearied of her."[21] He thanked her for the gumbo and left. But if he was not attracted, neither was he unadmiring: "I thought her intrepid; that lady had balls! She went after what she wanted the way a man does."[22]

A reader of Hellman's memoirs would learn very little about her love life. A few sentences about her marriage to Arthur Kober, much more about Hammett, here and there some brief allusions to other men: "R," for one, a passing reference to John Melby. Oddly, however, Hellman devotes a full chapter in her memoirs to a man who helped her financially, but rejected her sexually—Arthur Cowan, a rich Philadelphia lawyer whom she first met in the early 1950s. "I came to know his face as well as my own," she writes, implying a great intimacy.[23] Apparently Cowan liked being seen with Hellman, liked being part of her circle of celebrities. He offered to manage her money and promised to leave her money in his will. But he told her that she was too old for him; his preference was for young, beautiful women. "I wouldn't marry you, Arthur, I never even thought about it," Hellman recalls in her memoir. But she gives Cowan the last word in this exchange: "Like hell you wouldn't. . . . You'd marry me in a minute. Maybe not for anything but my money, but I'm not marrying you, see?"[24]

Hammett continued to be a presence in Hellman's life until, after a long illness, he died in 1961. When she came to write her memoirs she gave him a central place in her life story, and she presented theirs as a relationship of deep love and affection which, despite difficulties, had lasted a lifetime. But long before his death he had vacated his place in her sexual life, and in the hopes she had for a permanent partner.

Hellman had not yet given up hopes of Blair Clark when Peter Feibleman came into her life. Hellman first knew Feibleman as a ten-year-old boy in New Orleans, the son of friends. When she met him again he was a handsome published writer in his late twenties. Hellman took an interest. "I have had a fine, a rare, a desired and almost forgotten kind of voyage— the discovery of my feelings for an interesting man," she wrote him after a meeting in Los Angeles.[25] Eventually they became lovers, at least for a time. Feibleman was twenty-five years her junior.

No relationship with Hellman was simple. Feibleman soon understood that her needs could consume him. He insisted on his own life, with people of his own age. He insisted that they live separately most of the time. He wrote her: "Here it is once more: I don't want to live together, Lilly, not on a permanent basis. I need other people too much, and I need to make a life. . . . We have a shot at a new kind of friendship now, let's not muck around with it, Lilly."[26]

Hellman tried to appear reasonable, but she had little control of her emotions. She hired a detective to find out who Feibleman was seeing; she falsely complained to him of receiving threatening telephone calls from one of his girlfriends. She listened in on his telephone conversations, and when she was caught, she exploded in moral outrage . . . *"imagine your accusing me of such a thing . . ."* I "realized," Feibleman wrote, "that Lilly's almost legendary sense of justice, the justice upon which so much of her life was based, was the justice of a child . . . It didn't matter when the man had truly broken the rules of the relationship, any more than it mattered what those rules were, as long as she felt something had been done against her. It was sandbox thinking . . . The biggest difference between Lillian as a grown-up and Lillian as a child was that she was taller."[27]

It didn't please Hellman that sex between them ended as she grew older and sicker. But Feibleman cared for her and remained in her life until the end. Hellman had lucked out, and so had Feibleman. When Hellman died she left him her house on the Vineyard, and enough money to live on for the rest of his life.[28]

8

—⋙⬧◆⬧⋘—

Counterparts

LILLIAN HELLMAN must have loved her Julia. No other such entirely admirable character exists in her work, except, perhaps, for "Kurt Muller," the hero of *Watch on the Rhine*. Like Julia, Kurt is a heroic anti-Fascist.

In her memoir *Pentimento*, Julia is presented to the reader as Hellman's cherished friend, her oldest and dearest friend. Hellman has loved Julia since girlhood. She loves Julia for her intelligence, her bravery, and her beauty, for her nobility of spirit, not for her riches, although it so happens that Julia is very rich.

After an idyllic girlhood together, life has parted the friends. When both girls are nineteen, Julia leaves New York, first to study at Oxford, and then to go to Vienna where she hopes to undergo a training analysis with Freud himself. Hellman marries and goes to Hollywood, where she meets Dashiell Hammett and becomes a playwright.

As Hellman tells the story, she next sees Julia in 1934. Hellman has traveled to Paris to work in solitude on *The Children's Hour*. In Paris, she gets a telephone call telling her that Julia is in a hospital in Vienna. Hellman rushes to Vienna. Julia is not in good shape. Her beautiful is face covered in bandages, and there is something very wrong with her leg. We are told that Julia is a Socialist; in synchrony with her beliefs she has been living in a one-room apartment in a Vienna slum, indifferent to her great inherited wealth, except as it can be used to help the Austrian workers in this year after the Nazis have taken power. On occasion, Hellman tells us, she has also used her money to show her love for her dear friend, Lillian, by buying her expensive antiques.

Julia is in the hospital because she has been wounded by the Fascist troops of Engelbert Dollfuss. At Julia's insistence, Hellman leaves her in Vienna and does not see her again until 1937, when she is once again in Paris and is asked to smuggle money to Julia in Berlin so that Julia may continue her anti-Fascist work. We now learn what was wrong with Julia's leg: it was amputated in the Vienna hospital.

Leaving aside the matter of Hellman being in Europe at all in 1934—her known schedule does not allow for the two months she says she spent there, working by herself on *The Children's Hour* in Paris, visiting Julia in Vienna for several weeks—it may occur to you that Hellman must have been of two minds about Julia, so savagely did she physically batter her, taking off Julia's leg, eventually killing her, and finally destroying the remains of Julia's beauty altogether by giving her corpse a hideously sewn together face, as she tells the story in *Pentimento*. Of course, things might just have happened that way.

Kurt Muller, the hero of *Watch on the Rhine*, also risks his life for the anti-Fascist cause, and he has bullet scars on his face and broken bones in his hands to show for it. But when we leave him in Hellman's play, he is still alive, still handsome, still united with his beloved wife and children. And although he is going back into the Nazi maw, Hellman has at least given him the possibility of surviving the war.

All of her life, Hellman stood by the reality of Julia, but the argument about whether Julia existed as Hellman's friend was resolved long ago, and not in Hellman's favor. We can take it as given that Hellman invented her. If not exactly invented her, then, rather like a cuckoo in reverse (or a writer of fiction) she raided another bird's nest to incubate and raise an unrelated hatchling as her own.

Muriel Gardiner, whose life Hellman had appropriated to create her "Julia," wrote Hellman a gracious letter a few years after "Julia" was published:

> Ever since your beautiful book Pentimento appeared, friends and acquaintances have been asking me whether I am Julia. Unlike your Julia, I am—obviously—still alive, and I have not been wounded and my daughter lives with her family in Aspen, Colorado. But many other things in Julia's life agree with mine. . . . I have never met you, though I heard of you often through our good friend, Wolf Schwabacher . . . and I have seen and admired many of your plays and enjoyed your books.
>
> I hope you do not find this letter an intrusion. There is no need to answer it. I often thought of writing you before, but did not want to bother you. Now, however, several more recent friends have again asked "Are you Julia?"[1]

Hellman did not answer this letter. When it became publicly known that Gardiner had written it, Hellman said that she had no memory of having received it.

Although Hellman always publicly denied it, we know now that from at least 1938 through 1940—the period in which Hellman set *Julia*, and during which she wrote *Watch on the Rhine*—Hellman was a member of the Communist Party.[2] It hardly matters whether she was an actual member or a fellow traveler.

Anyone might have deduced her sympathies from hearing her speak from public platforms, from the groups she belonged to, from the petitions she signed; all of which ardently supported and defended the policies of the Soviet Union as the American Communist Party understood them.

But those particular years, encompassing as they did the period of the Hitler-Stalin pact, were a litmus test of Party loyalty. There were Communists who could not stomach the sight of the Swastika flying over Moscow airport on the day the Pact was signed; Communists who could not fathom the Party's sudden lack of interest in the anti-Fascist groups in which Communists had been encouraged to be active; who could not join the Party's applause of Stalin's strategic cleverness in signing the Pact. Many Communists left the Party at that moment. Hellman remained, as did Hammett.

When Hellman sat down to write "Julia," thirty years had passed since the events she was recounting. Memories had faded with the decades: there were new wars, new political movements. In describing Julia as a Socialist, Hellman may simply have wanted to present Julia as a person with generic leftist sympathies, assuming that her readers would not know about the deep schisms between Socialists and Communists in the 1930s. But Hellman, herself, would have known that a Socialist or a Social Democrat, would not have shared her own commitment to Stalin and his policies. And since Julia's work was saving the lives of those threatened by Nazism, we can assume that she would have been appalled and frightened by the Nazi-Soviet Pact. She would have been appalled, that is, had Hellman allowed her to live long enough. Unfortunately, or conveniently, as far as Hellman's story goes, Julia was killed off by her author in 1938, before the Pact was signed.

As it happens, however, we do know what Julia's avatar, Muriel Gardiner, thought about Stalin and the Soviet Union.

In her own memoir, published the year before Hellman died, Gardiner reflects on the state of the world in 1937: "Nazi power was growing, Nazi threats were increasing. . . . In Russia, Stalin had long since destroyed early hopes that anything resembling socialism could ever be achieved there."[3]

Gardiner knew war was coming. In 1939, she took her family to Paris. While they waited for the ship that would get them out of Europe and back to the United States, "The Hitler-Stalin nonaggression pact was signed," Gardiner wrote. "Joe and I, alone at home, heard it on the radio. It was something I had never foreseen or imagined. I wept. I had believed myself free of any illusions about the Soviet Union, but I must still have had some lingering belief that Communism was not so appalling as Nazism. Now the two had practically become one."[4]

In the spring of 1939, before the Pact was signed, Hellman had completed a first draft of her unequivocally anti-Nazi play, *Watch on the Rhine.*[5] In April 1941, while the Pact was still in force, the play was staged: an act of literary dissent from the Party line; and predictably, the play was attacked by *The Daily Worker.* Even Hammett told Hellman that she had ruined a great play by "anti-Fascist sentimentalism."[6] On the other hand, despite having a play running on Broadway that exhorted Americans not to be passive in the face of Nazi aggression, Hellman attended the Fourth National Congress of the League of American Writers in early June of that year. She and Hammett, in accord with the program of the Congress, urged America to stay out of the war. It was, then, surely something of a relief to Hellman when, on June 22nd, Hitler turned his armies on the Soviet Union. "The Motherland has been attacked!" she dramatically announced to her friends Sidney and Beatrice Buchman.[7]

If Hellman had never known the woman on whom she modeled Julia, the character of Kurt Muller was based on a man whom Hellman knew quite well. This was Otto Katz, the Czech-born Jew who had urged Hellman to go to Spain. In Spain, she and Katz had an encounter, which she recorded in a diary entry for October 28, 1937:

> "You don't look well, Otto. Is something the matter?"
>
> "Ach. I've been sick for years. In my forties I am an old man."
>
> "It must be hard to be a Communist."
>
> "Yes. Particularly here."
>
> "How long have you been [a Communist]?"
>
> "I can't remember, it's so long ago. A young boy, almost a child."
>
> He got up and took my arm and pressed it hard. "Don't misunderstand. I owe it more than it owes me. It has given me what happiness I have had. Whatever happens I am grateful for that."[8]

This is a remarkable dialogue, virtually bereft of information, yet heavy with meaning; and, as it turned out, strangely prescient.

For one thing, what did Katz mean by saying that he found it particularly hard to be a Communist in Spain? Hellman seems to understand him, but keeps her reader in the dark. Perhaps it was the fact that Katz, as a Comintern agent, would surely have known that the purges then taking place in Moscow had spread to Spain. *Pravda* had recently reported that "the purging of the Trotskyists and the Anarcho-Syndicalists has begun; it will be conducted with the same energy with which it was conducted in the U.S.S.R."[9]

And the prescient part of Katz's conversation—his gratitude for the happiness "it" had given him: *Whatever happens I am grateful for that* . . . Did he actually anticipate what was to happen? Or was that Hellman's flourish to her diary entry?

By the time Hellman wrote *An Unfinished Woman* thirty years later, she knew what had happened to Otto Katz. She knew that after the Second World War he had returned to Czechoslovakia, and that in 1952 he was arrested, along with thirteen other high-ranking members of the Czech Party and government, most of them Jews. He was tortured, as they all were. At the trial, known to history as the Slansky trial, named for Rudolf Slansky, General Secretary of the Czech Party, Katz confessed: "For thirty years I defended bourgeois ideology, disrupted the unity of the working class." He admitted to charges of Trotskyism, Titoism, and particularly Zionism and to being a saboteur and a traitor to his country.[10] Eleven of the fourteen defendants were Jewish; a distinct point was made in their indictments of their "Jewish origin." Eleven of the fourteen, Katz among them, were executed.[11]

We do not know what Hellman thought or said in 1952 when she heard of Katz's arrest and execution. However, in 1968, she added a note to her diary entry of their 1937 conversation: "[1968 When I read of his execution in Prague . . . I remembered the passion with which he spoke that night and hoped that it carried him through his time in jail, his day of death]."

For a woman ordinarily moved to outrage by the smallest injustice, this seems a very cool reflection. And it does seem too much for even irony to bear that in the end it wasn't the Nazis that Hellman's Kurt Muller had to fear.

9

The Incurious Tourist

IN THE spring of 1944, Hellman's fifth play, *The Searching Wind*, opened on Broadway. In ten years as a playwright, Hellman had produced five plays, four of them successful. Hellman was not yet forty, audiences waited for her next play, she was a singular force in the American theater, and she had friends in high places. In January 1942, little more than a month after Pearl Harbor, *Watch on the Rhine* was selected for a "command performance" at the White House. Hellman chatted at dinner with Franklin Roosevelt. Two years later, in the third year of the war, Hellman's stature as a cultural figure, and her well-known political sympathies, resulted in an invitation to the Soviet Union where Stalin offered to see her, she said.

Lillian Hellman landed in Moscow on November 5, 1944, and would remain in the country for two-and-a-half months. She felt herself to be an unofficial cultural ambassador to our wartime ally. It is not clear exactly who sanctioned her trip, but given wartime travel restrictions, there was certainly some governmental sanction, the president, himself, perhaps, or his close advisor Harry Hopkins.

What was Hellman expected to do for the war effort? The Second Front had been launched; although military victory was still six months off, it was clear at that moment that the Allies would win the war in Europe. Diplomatic relations between Roosevelt, Churchill, and Stalin were tense: Stalin was suspicious as ever of his temporary allies; and the Western leaders, while deeply concerned about Stalin's territorial ambitions in Europe, were aware that they could do little to prevent Stalin's eventual control of the Balkans, Poland, and the Eastern European states.

Not long before Hellman arrived in Moscow, Vice President Henry Wallace had been sent on a tour of Siberia. Whether from diplomatic tact, or the efficiency of his guides, Wallace never noticed that he was in the middle of the Gulag. He told his hosts that the landscape reminded him of our great Wild West.[1] In Hellman's case, it was perhaps thought that another visitor friendly to the Soviet Union might help allay Stalin's suspicions of the West. And, indeed, Hellman proved to be a benign presence in Moscow. She lived, primarily, at Spaso House, the Ambassadorial residence then occupied by W. Averell Harriman. Harriman liked Hellman; he found her entertaining. He knew that she had a particular interest in the Soviet Union and assumed that she would be a lively participant in dinner table discussions, where he, George Kennan, and others at Spaso House who were deeply knowledgeable about Soviet Russia argued Stalin's policies and their implications for post-war Europe. But Hellman could not be drawn into serious conversations, although she often endured "baiting" for her views: "It tended to become Miss Hellman vs. the field," said her lover, John Melby, "and I know she was often personally and deeply offended."[2] For her part, Hellman wrote that she found the atmosphere of Spaso heavy and gloomy. She preferred the more informal atmosphere of the Metropole Hotel, and the rowdier company of foreign journalists and international riff-raff.

Hellman was an admired writer in Russia. The Soviet Foreign Office offered her the extraordinary privilege of relative freedom of movement. In fact, officials insisted on sending her to places she did not really want to go—to Leningrad, and to the front lines—while Hellman's preference was to remain in Moscow where her days and nights were full. She began her intense love affair with John Melby. She made friends with Kathleen Harriman, the Ambassador's daughter, who found her "great fun" to have around, and "very enthusiastic about Russia."[3] She fulfilled her cultural responsibilities by making friends with Russian cultural figures, especially the great film maker, Sergei Eisenstein, whom she would see three or four times a week. She did agree to go to the recently besieged, starved city of Leningrad. She spoke with Russian writers, and became good friends with her young guide and translator, Raya Orlova, with whom she would keep in touch after she left the country. At the Metropole Hotel, she met *Time* reporter John Hersey, who became a lifelong friend and, to whose chagrin, Hellman, alone, of all the foreign journalists in Moscow, was given permission, indeed almost forced, to go to the Russian-Polish front.

When Orlova informed her of this exciting development, Hellman was not pleased. "It was not good news to me," she wrote. "I saw no point to the trip. I was not a journalist and didn't wish to report on the war. I was uncertain I could take the hardships with any grace, I was frightened."[4] But on December 27, she and Orlova were on a train, headed for Lublin.

Hellman made extensive notes during her 1944 stay in Soviet Russia. In one entry she mentions the antisemitism she encountered, which made her feel "like the Jewish shopkeeper during a pogrom rumor"; another entry notes "the deep reverence & respect that even intellectuals have for Stalin," and further elaborates on the theme of Russian intellectuals, as she understood their position:[5]

> The Russian intellectual has had a hard life. . . . The 1930's were the first promise of something better, but the promise was soon followed by the hurricane of the 1937–38 purges that sent him whirling. . . . The accusations against his friends or his heroes were only half understood. . . . Great honor must and will be paid those who did protest the criminal purges. It is hard to judge those who tossed about in silent doubt and despair, but it is even harder to believe that they did not understand what was happening.[6]

On the simplest level, Hellman is mistaken; she often tells us that she has a bad memory for dates, so perhaps she was confused between the 1920s, and 1930s. Hellman's friend Sergei Eisenstein could have told her, as he told Isaiah Berlin when they met in Moscow a few months after Hellman's visit, that the early 1920s was the time of relative freedom in the arts: "We were young and did marvelous things in the theatre. . . . It was terrific. Goodness how we enjoyed ourselves!"[7]

But even in that comparatively free decade, by the later 1920s Osip Mandelstam was barred from publishing in the Moscow press.[8] And by the early 1930s, when Stalin had worked himself into a position of unchallengeable power, Soviet artists were subjected to the strict orthodoxy of the Communist Party and to the policy of Socialist Realism in the arts. Even writers who had fled the Soviet Union in the 1920s could not imagine what was to come: "Could we at that time foresee the death of Mandelstam on a rubbish heap, the end of Babel . . . Party politics in literature aimed at destroying two if not three generations? Could we foresee twenty years of silence on Akhmatova's part? The destruction of Pasternak?" Nina Berberova wrote in her memoirs.[9]

In 1932, the Union of Soviet Writers was established, and all other writers' organizations dissolved. This newly formed organization decided which writers were to be published, which not; which were to have the privileges of good apartments, dachas, good medical care, which not; which were to be ostracized for writing that did not serve Soviet political ends. And thus, when the purges came, which writers were most likely to live or to die.

Hellman's further reflections on the subject of Russian intellectuals and the purges are more difficult to understand. What did she mean when she wrote of the "great honor" that "must and will be paid" to protesters of the "criminal purges"? Did she mean that the generation of artists who perished in the purges would eventually be rehabilitated by history? Because, in the American understanding of the word "protest," there were no Russian protesters, at least none who lived to tell about it. No citizens signed petitions against the purges, none demonstrated in Red Square, as protesters might in front of the White House in a liberal democracy. Nobody protested at all, except, as Isaac Babel said, in whispers, under the covers, in the dark.

It is difficult, too, to parse the story Hellman tells about a woman who came to visit her in Moscow, a translator of French and English poetry who has a "tense and twitchy" face. As Hellman describes her, the woman seems half-mad:

"Where is Akhmatova?" the woman demands of Hellman. She answers her own question: "Gone, gone, with so many others. What do you think of that? *What do you think of that?*" (In fact, the great poet Anna Akhmatova had not gone to her death or to the camps as so many others of her generation did; she miraculously, if miserably, survived until her natural death in 1966.)

Hellman replies to her interlocutor: "Is it so terrible? You told me only last week about the trouble Akhmatova has had—"[10]

And there, at the dash, Hellman breaks off her diary entry, leaving her reader mystified: What *happened* to Anna Akhmatova? What *were* her troubles? Hellman's visitor raves on, but Hellman leaves us none the wiser about the tragic life of Anna Akhmatova—her first husband shot by the Cheka, their son sent to the prison camps for years, her second husband sent to the camps, the poet herself silenced, not permitted to publish.

Neither do we learn anything about Osip Mandelstam, who is also mentioned by Hellman's half-mad visitor. Mandelstam, of course, was dead by then, having given up the ghost in 1938 while in transit to a Siberian prison camp. About Isaac Babel, Hellman's visitor is apparently silent, and Hellman does not mention him in her memoir. Many years later, however, she assured a friend that Babel had died of natural causes, a heart attack.

How can you say that, Lillian? asked her friend, the playwright William Alfred, who knew that Babel had been shot in 1940, after his arrest and brutal interrogation.

"Oh," Hellman replied, "I know a very charming man in the Russian foreign service who told me that he died of a heart attack."[11]

When she wrote the addendum to her memoirs in 1979, Hellman, with the benefit of more than thirty years' hindsight, returned to Anna Akhmatova's story, but only to add to the mystification:

> True, that I could not understand the treatment of Akhmatova and other intellectuals, but a woman writer who was a close friend of Akhmatova told me she wasn't quite sure what the beloved poet had done, if anything, to deserve her punishment, but something strange, perhaps personal, must have taken place.[12]

On the afternoon of December 27, 1944, Hellman and Orlova boarded a train headed west, through the Ukraine and then to Lublin and the front lines of the war. The Red Army was camped on the eastern bank of the Vistula River, about one hundred miles from Warsaw. If Hellman knew that the Warsaw Uprising had begun five months earlier, and was now in its death throes as she arrived at the Russian front, she didn't mention it then, or later. It is most improbable that she knew what Averell Harriman and George Kennan knew: That the Red Army had been ordered to wait passively, as Kennan wrote, "on the other side of the river" watching "the slaughter by the Germans of the Polish heroes of the rebellion."[13]

While the Russian army waited for Stalin's orders to march into Warsaw, 20,000 rebels of the Polish Home Army were killed by the Germans, along with 200,000 civilians. Stalin had demonized the Polish resisters as "power hungry adventurers and criminals."[14] It was his intention that no dissenters should be left alive to oppose Soviet hegemony when the Red Army marched into Poland. And, in fact, by early January, when the Red Army entered Warsaw, it was a razed and emptied city.

Hellman was forbidden to ask questions at the front; nor, it seems, would she have asked had she been permitted. As she said with some impatience to a Russian major who told her she was not to inquire about her location, or about battle actions: "How often can I tell you I don't give a damn, and wouldn't know a platoon from an army corps or maybe even a gun from a plane."[15]

Hellman and Orlova remained at the front for almost two weeks. In Lublin, on December 31, they celebrated New Year's Eve, with Władysław Gomułka and Bolesław Bierut, the Polish Communists designated by Moscow to establish the postwar government in Poland. In her own memoir, Orlova gives us a vivid description of New Year's Eve 1944–45 at the front lines: "An empty barrackslike building, long undecorated tables. A bowl of cabbage, a bowl of potatoes, another bowl of cabbage. And full size bottles of vodka between them. . . . no bread at all."[16]

Hellman was back in Moscow on January 9, and she and John Melby resumed their affair. A week later, Hellman writes, she received a telephone call from one of Stalin's aides telling her that Stalin had agreed to an interview with her. She said that she was sorry, but was afraid she couldn't make it, and she left Moscow the following day. Years later, asked by an interviewer why she had passed on that unique opportunity, Hellman replied that she had "never understood why one just wants to meet the great or the famous because they're great and famous . . . it seemed to me we would have nothing to say to each other."[17]

Hellman was insistent on the fact that she was not a historian or a journalist, and it is true that by training and temperament, she was neither. Nevertheless, she was an intelligent, ambitious woman, a professional writer, who, in 1944, happened to find herself on the front lines of history. It is scarcely conceivable that she would have turned down the chance to speak directly with Stalin, if, indeed, she had had such a chance.

No memoirist tells you everything, that would be impossible, of course. But it is unusual to feel, as one does with Hellman, a writer's *reluctance* to tell, a determination to evade. Especially when she is the one who raises the subject in the first place. Hellman is a writer. You would expect her to be interested in Russian writers. But in 1944 she drops some names of great Russian writers and turns quickly away from them, from their work, from the fate they suffered. When it would be appropriate to mention a significant historical event, she omits it, when it is unavoidable, she refuses to engage; she dissembles when approaching politically sensitive material, hedges, misleads. How is it possible, for instance, to take at face value Hellman's statement "that the truth is that I do not know if [Hammett] was a member of the Communist Party and I never asked him."[18] She may not have asked him because the question was unnecessary; as she tells us only a few lines later: "He was often witty and biting sharp about the American Communist party, but he was, in the end, loyal to them."[19]

As for Hellman, herself, she says that she and Hammett "had not shared the same convictions," but never does she mention in what ways their convictions differed.[20]

Sometime around 1960, Alfred Kazin accepted an invitation to take part in a cultural event in Moscow. He arrived along with a group of American writers, none of whom were well-known enough to impress their Russian hosts. The Russian officials wanted to know: "Where is your Hemingway . . . [where is] . . . your great progressive dramatist and friend of people's democracies Lillian Hellman?"[21] The Russians had no problem saying of Hellman what she would not say of herself.

10

Lillian Hellman's Analyst

In the 1930s psychoanalysis was in high vogue in New York's artistic circles. Many of Hellman's friends were being analyzed by the fashionable Dr. Gregory Zilboorg. George Gershwin was treated by Zilboorg, as was Gershwin's mistress, Kay Swift; Ralph Ingersoll, Hellman's one-time lover, was a patient of Zilboorg's, and so were Herman Shumlin and Arthur Kober. Hellman, herself, began her analysis with Zilboorg in 1940, and continued to see him both as analyst and friend until the late 1950s.

Zilboorg was a short, stocky man, Jewish, born in Kiev in 1890. A photograph of him taken in the 1940s shows him to have a high, balding forehead, a thick moustache that does not quite reach the outer corners of his mouth and hangs in a deep fringe over his upper lip. He wears a bow tie, and rimless glasses that magnify dark, intense eyes.

Eventually, there would be questions about Zilboorg's biographical and professional claims: Was he actually part of the pre-revolutionary Kerensky government of Russia? Did he attempt to fight off the Bolsheviks? A more serious problem was whether or not he was licensed to practice medicine in New York State, since no record of a medical license issued to him could be found. But these questions did not arise until later. In 1931, Zilboorg opened a private practice as a psychiatric analyst, working from his home in the East Seventies in New York City.

There seems to be no question that Zilboorg was a man of great charisma and brilliance. He spoke three languages, including his native Russian. He had taught himself English within a few months of arriving in America, and he translated books from Russian into English. He wrote respected books himself, and was a co-founder of the *Psychoanalytic Quarterly*.

There are many stories about Zilboorg's treatment methods. He often discussed his patients and the disclosures they made to him with his other patients, many of whom were known to one another. He traveled with his patients on vacations, went to parties at their homes. He had definite ideas about how his patients should run their lives. For instance, both George Gershwin and his mistress, Kay Swift, were in treatment with him. When Swift wanted to divorce her husband, Zilboorg forbid her to do so. He also insisted that Swift, a very attractive woman, needed to have sex with him during their sessions; this activity, he said, was part of her treatment, for which she was naturally required to pay as usual. Zilboorg charged a great deal of money for his services. He charged Hellman seventy-five dollars an hour, the equivalent of about $700 in today's money.

George Gershwin came to Zilboorg with a number of physical problems; Zilboorg dismissed them as the symptoms of a neurotic, and when Gershwin suddenly died of a brain tumor in 1937, some of Zilboorg's colleagues believed that Zilboorg was to blame for a faulty diagnosis.

In 1942, a couple of Zilboorg's patients who felt that he had manipulated them, and taken advantage of them financially, complained about him to the Board of the New York Psychoanalytic Society. A Motion of Censure against Zilboorg was presented to the members. It failed to pass, and Zilboorg continued in his profession well into the 1950s.[1]

Hellman first consulted Zilboorg because she was confused by her success and worried about her excessive drinking. Zilboorg may have helped her to cut down, but she continued to drink all her life. Zilboorg disapproved of her relationship with Hammett; he preferred John Melby, whom he met several times, when Melby spent the summer of 1945 with Hellman in New York.

Like most analysands, Hellman, finally, did not know what to make of her analysis. The analytic process is so tortuous and mysterious, so much like magic, that in the end it requires a leap of faith. In 1967, almost ten years after Zilboorg had died, a Russian friend asked Hellman about her analysis:

"It was a long, painful business," Hellman said. "Then it's over and you can't fit the pieces together or even remember much of what you said or what was said to you. But I no longer have headaches."

Her friend then asks about Zilboorg, himself: "From one foreign quarter I hear that he was much respected . . . But from another I hear strange tales of his last years."

"Yes," Hellman says. "Zilboorg ended odd. . . . But I respected him and was grateful to him. . . . After he died it took me a long time to believe the ugliness I was hearing. I guess people who mesmerize other people die absolutely on the day they die—the magic is gone."

"Like Stalin," Hellman's Russian friend suggests.

"Yes," Hellman agreed. But she would like to excuse Zilboorg: "It was not all venality with Zilboorg," she says to her friend, "although it looked like that to many people." She thought that perhaps the financial scandals had something to do with Zilboorg's ideas about economic justice: "He was," she says, "an old fashioned Socialist who hated inherited wealth as undeserved, and many of his patients were people like that."[2] In other words, since Zilboorg's patients had inherited their money, it was legitimate that Zilboorg had bilked them of it, not for mercenary reasons, but for the sake of a political principle.

Hellman knew another psychiatrist, a friend, Dr. Milton Wexler, of whom she said that she counted on him to always tell her the truth.[3] After Hellman died, Wexler told an interviewer that the only thing Zilboorg had cured Hellman of was "a good deal of her money."[4]

11

◆┃◆┃◆

"You Are What You Are to Me"

So MUCH was at stake in the dark days of the Cold War—imprisonment, livelihood—that it was not unknown for friends to keep their distance from friends in trouble. When the writer, Jerome Weidman, heard that Dashiell Hammett was in jail for lack of $10,000 in bail money, Weidman called Arthur Kober and offered to put up the money himself.

"Are you out of your mind?" Kober said. "You're a married man. You have two children."[1] Kober, who had his own family and career to think of, did not offer to put up bail money for Hammett. Nor, it seems, did Lillian Hellman, although she preferred people to think otherwise.

In July 1951, four of eleven convicted Communist Party leaders jumped bail. Dashiell Hammett, a trustee of their bail fund, was called before the court and asked to reveal the whereabouts of the missing Communists, and also the names of contributors to the bail fund. He refused, and was found guilty of contempt of court. His bail was initially set at $10,000 (although, in the end, he was denied bail altogether and sentenced to six months in prison). In her 1951 diary, Hellman wrote of her distress on the day Hammett was sentenced: "The moral mess . . . should I, could I, wise, unwise, [to provide bail] Gregory [Zilboorg] advised not . . . The loss of head and too many consultations."[2]

Hammett and Hellman had gotten along remarkably well during the previous years. Hammett had been on the wagon since 1948. Even before that he had worked with her, had "given" her, in Hellman's words, *The Little Foxes* in 1946. In 1950 he worked with her again on *The Autumn Garden*, Hellman's homage to Chekhov, a play in which ten old friends gather at a summer guest house and speak bitterly of their lives and the roads not taken. The play opened in March 1951 to mixed reviews, and ran a respectable 101 performances.

Hammett was still trying to do his own work, but was as stalled as ever. That year he and Hellman spent their time together at Hardscrabble Farm, and at a rental house on Martha's Vineyard. Money was plentiful for both of them. Their relationship had survived Hammett's years of alcoholism, several years of wartime separation, numerous love affairs, and they had settled into what Hellman called "a passionate affection . . . the best time of our life together."[3] It had been a pleasant lull in the political storm, which hit Hammett first.

A two-page section of Diane Johnson's biography of Dashiell Hammett concerns itself with Hellman's behavior when she learned Hammett had been arrested. According to the account in Johnson's book, Hellman got the idea that Hammett's bail was set at $100,000, not $10,000. Trying to raise this large amount, she ran first to the Chase Bank intending to mortgage her townhouse, but learned that the paperwork would take too long. She then gathered up all her jewelry and went to a pawn shop, but was offered only $17,000. She phoned her friend William Wyler in Hollywood, who wired her money, but it was still not enough. Finally, she flew up to Martha's Vineyard where a friend mortgaged his own house for Hammett's bail. Finally she had enough money. Weeping in gratitude, Hellman flew back to New York only to learn that her efforts have been in vain and Hammett has been denied bail and must go to prison at once. But just as she is about to leave for the courtroom to be at Hammett's side as he is taken off in handcuffs, she is handed a note from one of his three lawyers:

> Do not come into this courtroom. If you do, I will say I do not know you. Get out of 82nd Street and Pleasantville. Take one of the trips to Europe that you love so much. You do not have to prove to me that you love me at this late date.[4]

Despite Hellman's best efforts to thwart Hammett's potential biographers after his death in 1961, biographies did appear. Finally Hellman authorized a biographer of her own, Diane Johnson, to write Hammett's life. Hellman agreed to make herself and materials available to Johnson, but with some provisions in the contract that, essentially, made Johnson dependent on Hellman's approval for the publication of the book.

Johnson's book was published in 1983. A year later Hellman, herself, died, and Johnson was free to write about some of the problems that arose in working with Hellman: "For instance," Johnson wrote, "at one point [Hellman] said she was stunned by a terrible omission in the manuscript: an account of her activities trying to raise bail for Hammett. . . . Since I had not dealt anywhere in the book with [these] activities . . . and since in any event he had not been granted bail, I had not included a discussion of her hypothetical or potential part in raising bail. But she insisted that this episode—proof as she saw it, of her love—be included, and the account was written by her and the book's editor."[5]

Had *any* of it happened? The half-crazed running around New York to banks and pawnshops? The flight to the Vineyard to raise the sum Hellman inflated from $10,000, which she easily could have raised, to $100,000? The note from Hammett's lawyers, which none of his three lawyers could recall delivering to Hellman?[6] The only verifiable incident in Hellman's story is that she did, indeed, quickly take off for Europe.

Lillian "had left almost immediately after the trial for Europe," Hammett's daughter Jo wrote. "I could tell [Papa] was surprised and hurt. But not angry. At least I didn't hear it in his voice . . . but what was really shabby was the note she later fabricated from my father's lawyer as justification. . . . The whole thing sounded so much like Lillian and so unlike Papa that it would have been funny if you were in a laughing mood."[7]

Dashiell Hammett came out of prison in December 1951, his health broken for good. Prison life had made him a much sicker man. He had hoped to recuperate at Hardscrabble Farm, but Hellman, facing a large tax bill, had put the farm on the market while Hammett was in prison. Legally, the farm was hers, but Hammett had considered Hardscrabble to be his as much as Hellman's: he had put a great deal of work and money into it, and had loved the place. "I haven't thought about it much," he wrote to Jo when Hellman was packing up the farm, "except to know it's going to leave quite a hole in life."[8]

Hammett wrote the above letter to Jo from his apartment on West 10th Street. Six months later, faced with a large tax bill of his own, one of well over $100,000, and the consequent attachment by the IRS of what income he had been making from his copyrights, Hammett could no longer afford the Village apartment. He moved to a small cottage owned by friends, in Katonah, New York, and lived there alone and fairly solitary for five years, still trying to write his novel, getting sicker by the day. By 1958 it was clear to him, and to his friends, that he could no longer physically manage on his own. He had emphysema, and may have already had the lung cancer that would kill him. He made plans to move into a Veterans Administration hospital. Hellman took him in then; in May, 1958, Hammett moved into Hellman's luxurious townhouse at 63 East 82nd Street.

For the next years Hellman arranged for Hammett's care, supported him financially, and saw him through to his death in January 1961. It was not an ideal arrangement for either of them. Not for Hammett who had always guarded his independence; not for Hellman, who often resented the burden of his illness, and who continued to want from him the emotional generosity he had always withheld. She was aware that when visitors came to see him, "there was warmth and need and maybe even the last weeks a sexual need, but not with me," she wrote in her diary. And, "sometimes now, I think he wanted to be good friends, but more often I know that he didn't."[9]

Hellman's moment of confrontation with the House Committee on Un-American Activities would come in May 1952. Many years later she wrote about it in powerfully dramatic terms in *Scoundrel Time*, the third in her volumes of memoirs. At the time, however, she came out of it very well: she did not name names, she was not cited for contempt, she did not go to jail. She was blacklisted in Hollywood and her income was diminished, but apart from that Hellman's life continued much as before. She traveled to Europe, she gave dinner parties, she had affairs. She continued to work, not in Hollywood, but on Broadway. In 1956, she adapted Jean Anouilh's play about Joan of Arc, which appeared on Broadway as *The Lark*, and was a great success. She collaborated with Leonard Bernstein on a musical version of *Candide*, which was not so much of a success. In 1960, she presented what turned out to be her last original play, *Toys in the Attic*. Here, again, she turned to family material, this time to her immediate family—to her father and mother, and her Hellman aunts—for a play about the destructive power of family, love, and money. *Toys* was a smash hit; it ran on Broadway for about a year and a half and won Hellman the New York Drama Critics' Circle Award for best play.

Hellman was forced to sell Hardscrabble Farm for back taxes, but the blacklist did not break her financially, as it did so many of her friends. In 1955 she was able to buy a house with three acres and a private beach on Martha's Vineyard.[10] She also held mortgages on various properties in New York that brought her income; she had stocks and bonds, jewelry and furs, and a well-staffed New York townhouse.[11] How strange, and yet how like her, to claim that in order to make ends meet she "took a half-day job in a large department store, under another name." No doubt she just wanted to underline the evils of the blacklist.[12]

In the spring of 1960, Jo Hammett flew to Martha's Vineyard with her family to see her father for what she knew would be a final visit. She found Hammett elegantly dressed but more debilitated than ever, thin, pale, and withdrawn. Jo stayed on the Vineyard for a week. Hellman complained to Jo about Hammett and the isolation his illness imposed on her; she hinted that perhaps Jo might take him home with her. But, Jo wrote, "When I was with him I saw nothing but kindness and patience from her. . . . I felt as close to her as I ever will. She had the burden of his care, didn't want it, but took it anyway. Much of what they had had together was gone—the fun, the sex, the fighting—but the love remained. I could be wrong about a lot of things with Lillian, but not about that."

One day during that visit, Jo "bumped into Lillian in the

village, and we went for coffee. . . . She went briefly into my father's sorry financial situation and told me she would be his executrix. Her final remark on the subject was cheerful, 'We won't fight about money, will we.' Not really a question but a confident prediction."[13]

Hammett had made his will in 1952. Jo, his favorite daughter, was to get half of his estate, Mary a quarter, and Hellman a quarter. Hellman was named as Hammett's executor.

Eight months after Jo last saw him Hammett died, owing the government, and other creditors, more than $220,000; of these debts, Hellman claimed $40,000 as "advances" she had made to Hammett during his lifetime. Hammett's copyrights, which were owned by his estate and his family, were his only assets. For purposes of probate, Hellman valued these at $1,000. When the government agreed to settle Hammett's debts by putting his copyrights up for public auction for whatever they would bring, Hellman and her lawyer friend, Arthur Cowan, were the sole bidders; they bought Hammett's copyrights for $5,000. This arrangement left Hammett's family with no legal claim on his work. At Cowan's death in 1964, Hellman became sole owner of Hammett's copyrights.

As Hellman had predicted, Jo did not contest Hellman's appropriation of her legacy, although this took some persuading on Hellman's part, but not much. Several letters between her and Jo were exchanged. Hellman suggested that in buying Hammett's copyrights she was saving Jo and Mary from inheriting their father's debts. This was not true; the government had already agreed to settle Hammett's tax liabilities for the amount of the copyright sale. Hellman's lawyers sent Jo and Mary waivers of their interest in the Hammett estate, and they signed away their rights to what they believed was an estate without monetary value.

But almost immediately after his death many of Hammett's copyrights were renewed by Hellman, and Hammett's work began to make money. In 1961 his novels were re-issued in paperback, and have remained in print ever since. An edition of his stories *The Big Knockover*, with Hellman's introduction, was published in 1966. His novel *The Dain Curse* was sold for a television mini-series for $250,000. Hellman and her literary agents managed everything and kept everything. When Jo was asked by William Wright, one of Hellman's biographers, if Hellman had ever given her any of the money earned by her father's work, she said, "Maybe a fifty dollar check at Christmas." Jo's mother was still alive at the time, and Jo said that "the only negative thing I remember my mother saying about Lillian was that she thought Lillian should have given Mary and me some of my dad's things after his death." [14]

Jo displayed no bitterness or anger: "I figured that Lillian was my father's wife for all practical purposes, and that she was entitled to a widow's rights."[15] Not until Hellman's death in 1984 did Jo receive her inheritance, but not in full even then. Jo had to hire a lawyer to wrest Hammett's copyrights from a trust Hellman had established to control them after her death.[16]

"Since [Hellman's] death last summer," Hammett's biographer Diane Johnson wrote, "I have reflected that had she died before [my] book was written, it might well have included a story it presently does not, an intriguing story of a powerful woman's struggle to possess and command at last the elusive ghost of a man about whom she was insecure in life. It is a story which seems to me to be about love, to be sure, but also about control, revenge, hate and money."[17]

Three years before he died, Hammett had written to Hellman: "There's a popular song called 'You're My Destiny' that has a second line I kind of like . . . 'you are what you are to me,' because it's got that nice kind of ambiguity . . ."[18]

12

---✦◆✦---

Having Her Say

IN FEBRUARY 1952, Lillian Hellman was handed a subpoena to testify before the House Committee on Un-American Activities: HUAC, as the Committee was generally known. By then, the Hollywood Ten, many of them well-known to Hellman and Hammett, had served jail terms for refusing to answer the Committee's questions about their affiliation with the Communist Party. Julius and Ethel Rosenberg had been tried, found guilty of espionage for the Soviet Union, and were in prison. Alger Hiss, who had denied giving State Department papers to the confessed Soviet agent Whittaker Chambers, was also in prison, convicted of perjury. Leaders of the Communist Party had been tried and jailed under the Smith Act for teaching and advocating the violent overthrow of the government. And Hammett, too, had served five months in prison, and had been released only two months earlier. Hellman was frightened when her subpoena arrived, but she was not surprised.

Hellman did not write about this time in her life until 1976, when she published her third memoir, *Scoundrel Time*. The intervening quarter-century did not mellow her memories or her judgment of that era in American life. If anything, as she writes in her addendum to the book, "I am angrier now than I hope I will ever be again; more disturbed now than when it all took place."[1] And indeed, Hellman's voice in the memoir—powerful, contemptuous, bitter, self-righteous—leaves no doubt of the sincerity of her feelings.

Scoundrel Time is essentially a classic morality tale. A decent woman, Hellman, innocent of any wrong-doing, is caught up in that uniquely ugly American moment known generally as McCarthyism. She is summoned to appear before HUAC, where a band of cynical, careering politicians is bent on exploiting and magnifying American fears of Russians abroad, and subversives at home. HUAC's method is to subpoena witnesses of known or suspected Communist affiliation and subject them to a kind of inquisition—a "degradation ceremony," as Victor Navasky has called it—to extract confessions of membership in the Communist Party, to name other Communists known to the witness, and to confess the details of subversive activities in which these Communists may have engaged.

When Hellman gets her subpoena, Hammett warns her not to do any foolish grandstanding. As he tells her, he knows that she is not psychologically equipped to tolerate prison life, and Hellman knows he is right. She does not want to go to jail. But under no circumstances will she give the Committee names. Nor does she want to invoke the protection of the Fifth Amendment against self-incrimination which, by its very wording, carries the implication that the witness has something to hide.

So Hellman finds a good lawyer. She buys an expensive new dress for courage. On her lawyer's advice, she writes a letter to the Committee that contains a phrase which will become more famous than anything else she has ever written: *I cannot and will not cut my conscience to fit this year's fashions* . . .

On May 21, 1952—the day of her appearance before HUAC—Hellman keeps faith with her moral code: she does not name names. But, somewhat to her shame, she does not have the nerve to tell the Committee to go to hell. Instead she takes her lawyer's advice and invokes the Fifth Amendment when refusing to answer some questions she is asked about her membership in the Communist Party.

But the result of her appearance is all that she had hoped. Not only is Hellman *not* sent to jail, but her eloquent letter, which includes an offer to answer questions about her own views and activities as long as she is not required to name others, is read into the record and distributed to the press. From that moment on, she is almost universally applauded as a heroine. In *Scoundrel Time* she does not shy from presenting herself as such.

Scoundrel Time is not concerned only with Hellman's triumph. If she is the hero, who are the scoundrels? They are not, as one might imagine, the members of HUAC, or even Senator McCarthy, himself. Nor does the appellation apply to Elia Kazan and Clifford Odets and Budd Schulberg, witnesses who did name names before HUAC. These people are beneath Hellman's contempt. Her bitterness and anger are reserved for those who were in no danger from the Committee—the anti-Stalinist Left—the liberals, socialists, intellectuals who had broken with Stalin and with Communism in the 1930s.

"I had," Hellman writes, "up to the late 1940s believed that the educated, the intellectual, lived by what they claimed to believe: freedom of thought and speech, the right of each man to his own convictions, a more than implied promise, therefore, of aid to those who might be persecuted. But only a very few raised a finger when McCarthy and the boys appeared! . . . Many of them found in the sins of Stalin Communism—and there were plenty of sins and plenty that for a long time I mistakenly denied—the excuse to join those who should have been their hereditary enemies." Hellman went further in characterizing her scoundrels. Money and success had corrupted these "children of timid immigrants" who had made it so good "that they are determined to keep it at any cost."[2] It was clear to everyone who read those words, and the words that followed, that Hellman did not have in mind the children of Italian immigrants or Irish immigrants or Spanish immigrants.

In any case, it is in the nature of morality tales that the scoundrels do not get to tell their side of the story: "To hell with the fancy reasons they give for what they did," Hellman writes.[3] "If I stick to what I know, what happened to me, and a few others, I have a chance to write my own history of the time."[4]

And this she did, perhaps with more clarity than she intended. Whatever the Cold War was on an international level, "The real Cold War at the intellectual and cultural level," as Tony Judt observed, "was not fought between the Left and the right but *within* the Left. The real political fault line fell between communists and fellow traveling sympathizers, on the one side, and social democrats, on the other side."[5]

There can be no doubt on which side of the fault line Hellman stood. Although she denied it in her memoirs, and repeated the denial on all public occasions, in a privileged communication to her lawyer Joseph Rauh, Hellman acknowledged that she had been a member of the Communist Party from 1938 through 1940.[6] From her actual testimony before HUAC we can infer a somewhat longer period of membership. In answer to questions about whether she had been a member of the Communist Party in 1950, 1951, and, in the current year of 1952, she answered with a straightforward, "No, sir." Asked about previous years, she refused to answer.

But even if we accept as true Hellman's report of two years of Party membership, we also know that from the mid-1930s

through at least 1949, she never strayed far from Party pre-
cincts. Through the Cold War years of a Moscow-launched
peace movement ("the most notable success scored by international communism in the field of propaganda was its virtual
expropriation of the word 'peace'"), Hellman's voice was in-
fluential in many groups that were fronts for the Communist
Party.[7] The most significant of these was the Progressive Party's
1948 campaign for Henry Wallace's run for the presidency, in
which Hellman headed "Women for Wallace." The campaign,
the Progressive Party, itself, was dominated by the Communist
Party, as Hellman well knew, and as she says she told Wallace
when he asked. A year later Hellman was a prominent sponsor of the Waldorf Conference for World Peace, a gathering
that, as Murray Kempton wrote, was notable "as a discussion
between Americans who spoke critically of their government
and Russians who could hardly have offered theirs any such
treatment and safely gone home."[8]

Since Hellman names few of her "Scoundrels," we might
ask who they were, and what they eventually said in their own
defense. Among others, they included Sidney Hook, Diana and
Lionel Trilling, Mary McCarthy, Elizabeth Hardwick, Dwight
MacDonald, William Phillips, Murray Kempton, Irving Howe,
John Dos Passos, James T. Farrell, Alfred Kazin. Some had
once been close to, but had never joined, the Party; some were
disillusioned former Party members. What was true of them all
was that by the late 1930s, the purges, the Soviet manipulation
of the Spanish Civil War, the Pact with Nazi Germany had left
them bitterly disillusioned with the idea of a Soviet workers'
paradise. Most, though not all, remained on the Left, identi-
fying themselves as liberals or socialists, or social democrats.
Post-war events only confirmed their understanding of Soviet
policies: the annexation by the Soviet Union of Latvia, Lithu-
ania, Estonia, Western Ukraine; the brutal imposition of Mos-
cow-controlled governments in Poland, Hungary, Romania,

Albania; the Soviet blockade of Berlin; the Communist coup in Czechoslovakia; the show trials in Albania, Bulgaria, Hungary, and Czechoslovakia; the murderous anti-Semitic campaign that emerged in the Soviet Union in the late 1940s and which lasted until, mercifully for all, Stalin died.

In *An Unfinished Woman* and in *Pentimento*, Hellman had written almost exclusively about people who were dead, or, like "Julia," heavily disguised. No one had yet publicly emerged from these memoirs to say her nay. But although she named almost no one in *Scoundrel Time*, she was dealing with still-living history which teemed with living witnesses who had a strong stake in the events she described.

Dwight MacDonald, for one, who at various times in his life had described himself as an anarchist, a Trotskyist, a socialist, and who profoundly disagreed with Hellman's politics, but had kept on friendly terms with her over the years. Soon after the publication of *Scoundrel Time*, he was asked what he thought of the book:

"I thought it was an absolutely disgusting book . . . a silly book and also a very dishonest book. . . . She gives this self-dramatizing impression that she was isolated, that liberals didn't help her, that nobody helped her . . . if you read the book you'll see that all through everybody is on her side. Not politically, but for civil liberties . . . What she means is that nobody is on her side as a Stalinist."[9]

And this was true of Hellman's main defender, her lawyer, Joseph Rauh. When Hellman found herself with subpoena in hand she consulted several liberal lawyers and chose Rauh, an exemplary anti-Stalinist liberal, a founding member of Americans for Democratic Action, an organization that excluded Communists from membership. Rauh later explained: "The Communists would say: 'You don't believe in civil liberties because you're against us'; and then we'd say, 'Well, we're not against you and we'll defend your civil liberties to the extreme, but we don't think we have to have your crowd wreck our organization for us.'"[10]

Rauh's representation of Hellman was wholehearted. He explained the law to her. If Hellman did not want to name names, or to open herself to a charge of contempt, thus risking a jail sentence, she had to take the Fifth Amendment. By 1952, taking the Fifth was the strategy of choice for many of HUAC's witnesses who wanted the outcome Hellman wanted— no names, no jail. What gave Hellman's case its distinction was Rauh's stroke of genius, which had nothing to do with the particulars of Hellman's situation, but with Rauh's use of public relations—her letter to HUAC.

Her famous letter went through many drafts, written by Rauh and Hellman both. Hellman's were the memorable, ringing phrases. The most famous: *"I will not cut my conscience."* And: *"I am not willing now or in the future to bring bad trouble . . . to hurt innocent people who I knew many years ago in order to save myself is to me inhuman indecent and dishonorable."*

The letter continued in a distinctly un-Hellman-like tone of humility and unlikely references:

> I was raised in an old-fashioned American tradition and there were certain homely things that were taught to me. To try to tell the truth, not to bear false witness, not to harm my neighbor, to be loyal to my country. . . . In general I respected these ideals of Christian honor. . . . It is my belief that you will agree with these simple rules of human decency and will not expect me to violate the good American tradition from which they spring. I would, therefore, like to come before you and speak of myself . . .
>
> I am prepared to waive the privilege against self-incrimination and to tell you anything you wish to know about my views or actions if your committee will agree to refrain from asking me to name other people. If the Committee is unwilling to give me this assurance, I will be

forced to plead the privilege of the Fifth Amendment at the hearing.

As Rauh well knew, HUAC would never allow a witness to set her own terms for questioning. But, by a stroke of luck, the Committee blundered; during Hellman's testimony a Committee member agreed to make her letter part of the record, and at that moment it became a public document. Rauh was prepared on the spot to distribute copies to the press in the hearing room. The next day's headlines reflected his effectiveness: "Lillian Hellman Balks House Unit."[11]

Years later Rauh told Hellman's biographer Carl Rollyson how Hellman's case had differed from that of another of his clients, Arthur Miller, who had eschewed the Fifth Amendment and stood on his rights under the First Amendment: "[Miller] just was not going to tell them what the hell the names of other people were. If he went to jail, so be it."[12] Rauh admired Hellman, but he thought that Miller's was the more moral position, the more courageous position. It is also true that when Miller testified in 1956, the political hysteria had cooled several degrees.

Rollyson then asked Rauh about the public perception of Hellman's "moral victory" over the Committee. Rauh was amused. "The fact is," he said, "she did have to plead the fifth amendment. There was no way out of it." Given Hellman's condition that she would not go to jail: "She could have gone to jail if she had talked about herself, not pleaded the fifth amendment, then refused to answer questions about others." And about the accuracy of *Scoundrel Time*, Rauh said, "I would say it is Lillian's dramatization of it. I don't want to say anything that throws doubt on her veracity . . . But when she got done with [the story], it was better than a Babe Ruth home run."[13]

When *Scoundrel Time* was published in 1976, Hellman was very pleased with the good reviews and the success of the book—four months on the *New York Times* best-seller list, *Time* Magazine's description of her as "an invaluable American."[14] She assumed that she had had her say. But as the months went by, other critics made their way into print. Hellman's version of history was not to pass unchallenged.

Murray Kempton was concerned with the hypocrisy of the Communist devotion to civil liberties. He wondered, ironically, what Dashiell Hammett "might have said to Miss Hellman on the night he came home from the meeting of the board of the Civil Rights Congress which voted to refuse its support to James Kutcher, a paraplegic veteran who had been discharged as a government clerical worker because he belonged to the Trotskyite Socialist Workers Party. But then," Kempton noted, "Hammett was a Communist and it was an article of Party faith that Leon Trotsky, having worked for the Emperor of Japan since 1904, had then improved his social standing by taking employment with the Nazis in 1934."[15]

Sidney Hook's analysis of the heroine of *Scoundrel Time* was almost as long as the book itself, and fiercer in its disapprobation of Hellman than Hellman is of her scoundrels. Hook asks his readers to imagine the following:

> A woman of some literary talent and reputation who, although not a cardholding member of the Nazi German-American Bund . . . signs denunciations of the victims of Hitler's purges and frame-up trials as "spies and wreckers" . . . and characterizes the Nazi holocaust as a purely internal affair of a progressive country.[16]

Irving Howe wrote: "Surely Miss Hellman must remember . . . that there were old fashioned liberals like Henry Steele Commager and Roger Baldwin and old fashioned Socialists like Norman Thomas who combined a principled opposition to Communism with an utter rejection of McCarthyism. Thomas fought for the liberties of the very Stalinists who had supported the prosecution of Trotskyists in Minneapolis under the notorious Smith Act. . . . Those who supported Stalinism and its political enterprises . . . helped befoul the cultural atmosphere . . . helped to perpetuate one of the great lies of our century, helped to destroy whatever possibilities there might have been for a resurgence of serious radicalism in America."[17]

Hellman's opportunity to respond to her critics came when *Scoundrel Time* was republished with her other memoirs in 1979. But she had no taste for substantive debate and her arguments were *ad hominem*; she dismissed her critics as old fogeys, "people for whom the view from one window, grown dusty with time, has blurred the world and who do not intend ever to move to another window."[18]

She seemed unprepared to respond to Dan Rather, who, in a generally admiring CBS television interview in 1977, asked her: "Well, what about the charge that, while you could see what was wrong with McCarthy and that whole era in this country, you failed to see what was wrong with Stalinism?"

"I came to see what was wrong with Stalin—Stalinism—," Hellman replied. "I don't—I think it's fair enough to say that, at that period, I did not entirely see what was wrong with Communism. I happen never to have been a Communist for one thing, which is left out of this story. I don't quite understand that argument. I mean I don't really know what has— one—one thing has to do with another. I am—I was not a Russian, I was an American. . . . I was injured by McCarthy for one thing. I was not—I was personally not injured by Stalin."[19]

She thus walked right into the door Sidney Hook had left open: "Lillian Hellman . . . was not a German. Nor was she personally injured by Hitler. But she protested vigorously his terror regime . . . But then if the fact that she was not Russian and suffered no injury at Stalin's hands exonerates her from fail-

ure to criticize Stalin's crimes, why did she then defend them
. . . and defame those who . . . sought to establish the truth
about them?"[20]

"No one who did what I did, whatever his reasons, came
out of it undamaged," wrote Elia Kazan, who had named names
before HUAC. "Here I am thirty-five years later, still worry-
ing over it."[21] The Cold War fault line runs, perhaps, deeper
in Hollywood than anywhere else, where the entertainment in-
dustry had been a focus of the HUAC hearings. When Lillian
Hellman appeared at the 1977 Academy Awards, the entire audience rose to cheer her. When Elia Kazan was presented with
a Lifetime Achievement Award in 1999, several hundred members of his own generation stood outside the auditorium in protest: "Elia Kazan: Nominated for the Benedict Arnold Award,"
read one placard. Kazan's blacklisted contemporary Abraham
Polonsky remarked, "I hope somebody shoots him."[22] Inside
the auditorium some in the audience, of a younger generation,
refused to rise from their seats when Kazan walked on stage to
be honored.

Budd Schulberg had quit the Party in 1940. Some years
later he ran into Lillian Hellman at a cocktail party. As he recalled it, their conversation was hostile: He asked Hellman,
"What about Isaac Babel?"

"She said 'Prove it!' I told Lillian, 'Better writers than you
or me have been killed. She said, 'Prove it!' . . . I think it would
be very hard to get Lillian to criticize the death of a Soviet
writer. They could be stretched on the rack at Lubianka prison
and Lillian would go back on the ferry to Martha's Vineyard."[23]

In 1951, Schulberg named names before HUAC. He was
still thinking about that act shortly before his death in 2009
when he spoke about it to his son Benn: "It was not so black
and white. People don't understand how complicated it was.
I hated what McCarthy represented, and the Blacklist, but if

I was a Soviet writer I would have been killed too. We were attracted to socialist ideals, but in reality people were being murdered over there."[24]

Hellman was proud of herself, as she had a right to be. If she had not told the Committee to go to hell, as she would have preferred to do, and had reluctantly invoked the Fifth Amendment, still, by her own standards, and those of the people she respected, she had behaved impeccably: "I'm pleased with what I did in front of the House Un-American Committee," she told Marilyn Berger, who interviewed her for a television program in 1979. But she couldn't leave it at that. "Because," she added, referring to her offer to give the Committee information about herself, "it had good results and it led other people to take the same position, which was the first time anybody'd ever taken it."[25]

This last part of Hellman's sentence was not quite true. She had not been the first to offer the Committee information about herself while refusing to name names. At least one witness, the screenwriter Sidney Buchman, had done so months earlier. Hellman was, however, the first person, the only person who testified before HUAC, who was congratulated by a disembodied voice calling down to her from the press gallery: "Thank God, cried the ethereal voice, "somebody finally had the guts to do it."[26] To do what? The voice never specified. And no one else in the crowded Committee room that day could recall hearing it.

13

———◆◦◆◦◆———

Jewish Lit

"OUT OF the immigrant milieu there came pouring a torrent of memoir, fiction and autobiography," Irving Howe wrote of the explosion of Jewish writers into the mainstream of American literature. "Let us call this body of writing a regional literature—after all, the immigrant neighborhoods formed a kind of region."[1]

Hellman was the same age as Henry Roth, only ten years older than Saul Bellow, eleven years older than Bernard Malamud, but she knew almost nothing about the experiences on which they, and younger Jewish writers, drew. She had no immigrant parents or grandparents; she had not lived in the neighborhoods in which the children of immigrants were raised, had not known the struggle of these children to integrate into American life without breaking faith. "I wasn't brought up as a Jew," Hellman told an interviewer in 1981. "I know almost nothing about being one—I'm sorry to say—though not sorry enough to go to the trouble of learning. . . . I don't want it to alter my point of view about things."[2]

Hellman felt removed enough from the world of the immigrant's child so that in *Scoundrel Time* she could write of her betrayal by the children of "timid immigrants" as if she was describing a strange people.[3] When asked about that particular phrase, she denied that she had meant Jews. "No," she protested. "No. I'm a Jew, and I don't know how they could have thought a Jew could be snobbish about other Jews."[4] But she had gone too far in *Scoundrel Time* for plausible denial. Referring to the heads of Hollywood movie studios, and their cooperation with HUAC and the blacklist, she had concocted a contemptuous, if awkward, metaphor of Jewish timorousness: "Many of them had been born in foreign lands and inherited foreign fears. It would not have been possible in Russia or Poland, but it was possible here to offer the Cossacks a bowl of chicken soup. And the Cossacks in Washington were now riding so fast and hard that the soup had to have double strength and be handed up by running millionaire waiters."[5]

In October 1955, Dashiell Hammett wrote to his daughter Jo about the success of a new play adapted by Frances Goodrich and Albert Hackett: "[They] got smash-hit notices for the opening of their *Diary of Ann[e] Frank* and everybody is very happy about it—those that aren't jealous."[6]

Hellman was not jealous. She had been a part, if a minor part, of the success of the play. The Hacketts were old Hollywood writer-friends of Hammett's and Hellman's. They had adapted two of Hammett's *Thin Man* books for the screen, as well as *Father of the Bride* and *Seven Brides for Seven Brothers*. On the face of it, they were not an obvious choice to adapt Anne Frank's *Diary*. But Hellman had suggested them to Kermit Bloomgarden, another of her old friends, who was the producer of the play.

The story of how Anne Frank's *Diary* reached the stage is so tangled, Francine Prose writes, "so rife with betrayal and bad behavior, so mired in misunderstanding and complication," that after four books devoted to the subject, and more articles, it is still unclear exactly what role Hellman played in it.[7] What does seem clear is that at some point on the *Diary*'s road to Broadway, Hellman turned down the opportunity to adapt the work herself; she told the director, Garson Kanin, that should she write the script, the play would be so depressing it wouldn't run more than one night. It needed, she said, a "lighter touch."[8] According to Meyer Levin, who had been involved with the project from the start, and was the first to produce a script from the original diary, Hellman had been instrumental in blocking the production of his script, calling it "too Jewish."[9]

The Hacketts had some difficulties producing an acceptable script. On many weekends they flew to Martha's Vineyard to consult with Hellman, who made suggestions that Goodrich called "brilliant."[10] When the play became tied up in a lawsuit brought by Meyer Levin, Hellman denied that she had had a hand in the adaptation. The *New York Times* ran a story that indicated otherwise: "It turns out on the highest authority that Lillian Hellman had a considerable part in helping to fashion [The *Diary*'s] ultimate triumph. Miss Hellman, before she grabs the telephone or her typewriter to demand a retraction, had better pause. The credit was paid to her the other day by the play's adaptors themselves. . . . 'We don't know what we would have done without Lillian . . . '"[11]

The Diary of Anne Frank was a huge success in 1956 and received the Pulitzer Prize. With or without Hellman's help, the Hacketts had achieved a "lighter touch" by toning down the Jewish content of the *Diary*. The *New York Times* Sunday magazine noticed that "race and religion are incidental details of the drama."[12] Without the Hacketts' script, without Hellman's understanding of the nature of commercial theater, the play might never have been produced at all.

In some circles, however, the Hacketts' script was controversial and remained so. Forty years after the production of the play, Cynthia Ozick wrote: "Where the diary touched on Anne's consciousness of Jewish fate or faith, [the adaptors] quietly erased the reference or changed its emphasis. Whatever was specific they made generic." Ozick offers an example: Where Anne Frank had written: "if after all this suffering there are still Jews left, the Jewish people will be held up as an example . . . maybe our religion will teach the world and all the people in it about goodness, and that's the reason we have to suffer. . . . Through the ages Jews have had to suffer, but through the ages they've gone on living, and the centuries of suffering have only made them stronger." The Hacketts not only condensed the speech but changed its meaning. Anne's character says: "We're not the only people that've had to suffer. There've always been people that have had to . . . sometimes one race . . . sometimes another."[13]

If this was not a change Hellman had suggested, it was an idea she had often expressed. When Hellman wrote "Julia," in the 1970s, the character of Lilly asks Julia whether the money she has brought to Berlin will save Jews. Julia replies: "About half. And political people. Socialists, Communists, plain old Catholic dissenters. Jews aren't the only people who have suffered here."[14]

"Ironically," Tony Judt wrote, "the Jews of Eastern Europe and the Soviet Union achieved in the course of their extermination the equality that they had long since been promised . . . they became citizens, just like everyone else . . . killed as Jews, they were memorialized and officially remembered merely as the citizens of whatever country they happened to be in at the time of their death."[15]

The changes the Hacketts, Hellman, Kermit Bloomgarden, and Garson Kanin made to the diary were designed to "universalize" Jewish suffering, to make it not only palatable to the audience, but to ennoble the audience with a sense of participation in the grandeur of the human spirit. So that, in the Hacketts' version, a line plucked out of its context in the diary is placed at the very end of the play: As the footsteps of the Gestapo approach the attic in which Anne and her family are hiding, Anne, in the terror of that moment, incredibly cries out: *"I still believe in spite of everything that people are truly good at heart."*

Hellman's final Broadway play was an adaptation of a first novel by Burt Blechman called *How Much?* Renamed *My Mother, My Father and Me,* it opened on Broadway on March 21, 1963. Like *The Little Foxes* and *Another Part of the Forest,* it was about a family and money. Unlike the Hubbards, however, this family is unmistakable in its ethnicity: they are called the Halperns. What money the Halperns have, and it doesn't seem to be much, places them among the barely-hanging-on-nouveau riche. In this play Hellman is dealing with characters toward whom, in life, she felt only contempt.

Saul Bellow had liked the novel well enough to give it a blurb; some others among Hellman's friends were not at all sure why she had chosen it. It may be that she wanted to try her hand at the new "regional" literature. Bellow's *The Adventures of Augie March* had won the National Book Award in 1954; Bernard Malamud's stories *The Magic Barrel* won the same prize in 1959; Philip Roth's *Goodbye, Columbus* won it in 1960; Bruce Jay Friedman's very Jewish *Stern* was hailed as an "iridescent tour de force" when it was published in 1962. Hellman was a competitor by nature. Now she was about to try something new—an absurdist farce about Jews.

The story of *My Mother, My Father and Me,* such as it is, concerns a family of striving, first-generation New York Jews:

a weak father on the verge of bankruptcy; his ditzy wife who is a compulsive shopper and social climber; an immigrant grandmother; a son attempting to find himself by trying one fad after another. As Hellman wrote them, the Halperns are not characters so much as caricatures, set loose in a plotless play, with money as their motive power. The joke is on them, on their cluelessness and vulgarity. The play closed after seventeen performances.

"I thought, I think now, that it is a funny play," Hellman wrote, "but we did not produce it well and it was not well directed."[16]

There were other problems: Hellman's writing led Walter Matthau, who starred in the play, to tell her that he thought the play was anti-Semitic; others told her so as well. Hellman, herself, thought she was doing something brave: "It's time we had black and Jewish villains," she said. "Just because I'm a Jew doesn't mean I can't pick on Jews."[17] Or on niggers. The black housekeeper, Hannah, says to the Jewish grandmother: *Your daughter comes home, I say give me my wages and find yourself a Jew-type nigger.*"[18]

The play might have had more success with another writer, one with some sympathy for her characters. Hellman's dislike for the Halperns was palpable. But *My Mother, My Father and Me* had at least one fan who wrote Hellman in admiration: "This is a slashing fresh wind—a storm!—blown into the fetid air of our times . . . Marvelous—you are marvelous in your wrath."[19]

14

An Honored Woman

ALL THROUGH her middle years, honors came to Lillian Hellman: a Theater Arts Medal from Brandeis University; honorary doctorates from Wheaton College, from Smith, from Yale, from Columbia; election to the American Academy of Arts and Letters; two New York Drama Critics' Circle Awards. *An Unfinished Woman* won Hellman the prestigious National Book Award in 1969; *Julia*, the movie made from her story in *Pentimento*, won three Oscars in 1977.

By 1963, Hellman had come to an end of her work in the theater. When asked why she no longer wrote plays, she would answer variously that she had never felt entirely at home in the theater, or that she couldn't bear all the talk about the money it cost to produce a play. But, probably, she wasn't sure herself. Perhaps it was simply that she had begun working in the theater with Hammett, he was gone, and her run was over.

Even before she stopped working in the theater, Hellman

began to receive invitations to teach. She was invited to Harvard, to Yale, to Berkeley, to Hunter. She chaired seminars in writing and literature; she enjoyed it all and charmed her colleagues. A new life opened up to her, new friends presented themselves. She courted, and was courted by young people making their names—Susan Sontag, Renata Adler, Warren Beatty, Nora Ephron. Most of the young women fell away in time, as often happens in friendships between different generations, particularly when the older woman is needy and demanding, "burdensome," to Nora Ephron, "amusing company . . . [but also] a much feared bully" to Renata Adler.[1] Hellman's social life expanded even into Establishment circles: Jackie Kennedy came to dinner and brought McGeorge Bundy along; it seemed not to matter that the Bay of Pigs invasion, and the Vietnam war were Bundy's causes and Hellman's atrocities.

In the mid-1960s, Hellman began to think about writing her memoirs. She told an interviewer: "I was feeling bad about doing nothing and not knowing where to turn . . . And I'd done a great deal of magazine work and pieces through the years . . . I got out those pieces to see what I thought of them, and maybe I could make a collection of them. And I began to use those pieces and the diaries. . . ."[2] Hellman re-read her diary entries from wartime Moscow and was moved to make a trip to the Soviet Union.

In 1945, Hellman had left a Soviet Union still firmly ruled by Stalin. When she arrived in Moscow in October 1966, more than twenty years had passed since Stalin's death, ten years since he had been denounced by Khrushchev. During the Khrushchev decade the strictures on cultural life had been relaxed to such an extent that in 1962, Alexander Solzhenitsyn had been able to publish *One Day in the Life of Ivan Denisovich*. With Khrushchev's removal, the arrest, trial, and conviction of two Soviet writers, Andrei Sinyavsky and Yuli Daniel, who had published their work in the West, under pseudonyms, signaled that the thaw had come to an end. Sinyavsky and Daniel were sent to the camps, but the result was not what it had been in the Soviet past. Now, in the 1960s, not all Russian writers and intellectuals were frightened into silence; a dissident movement formed which could not be entirely crushed. Nor, any longer, could Soviet leaders count on the unwavering support of Communists and sympathizers in the West.

Hellman did not quite know what to make of this new Soviet Union. On the one hand she signed an open letter protesting the conviction of Sinyavsky and Daniel.[3] And, as she proudly wrote in her memoirs, her "oldest and best friends" in Russia "were now among the leading dissidents."[4]

Indeed, when she went to Moscow in 1966, she met Lev Kopelev, now the husband of Raya Orlova, her friend and translator from the old days. Kopelev had been imprisoned for ten years in Soviet camps for "fostering bourgeois humanism and compassion toward the enemy." In 1945, as a major in the Red Army, Kopelev had protested atrocities Russian soldiers were committing against German civilians. Raya and Kopelev introduced Hellman to their friend Alexander Solzhenitsyn, whom Kopelev had met in the camps. "I was impressed, of course, with Solzhenitsyn, but I cannot say I was attracted to the silent, strange figure. There was something out of order, too odd for my taste."[5]

There was some constraint between Orlova and Hellman as well. Their exchange of letters had ended not long after Hellman left Moscow in 1945. No matter that Orlova had been a lifelong and loyal Party member, her relationship with Hellman had made her suspect, and she had been summoned to the Lubyanka and interrogated over the course of an entire night: "They shouted at me, stamped their feet and humiliated me in every possible way," Orlova wrote in her memoirs. "They even asked: 'Is it true your father owned a Jewish shop?' I was afraid of them. . . . I came out onto Dzerzhinsky Square at daybreak.

. . . I had gotten off lightly."[6] After that, Orlova knew better than to answer Hellman's letters and she remained silent for twenty years.

The two women met again when Hellman arrived in Moscow in 1966. They were glad to see each other, but their understanding was not perfect. Orlova tried to speak with Hellman about Khrushchev's speech to the Twentieth Congress in 1956; she asked how Hammett had reacted to the revelation of Stalin's crimes. Hellman was curtly dismissive: "Raya, you always think that the world is revolving around your country. Nobody gives a damn about your Congress."[7]

For her own part, Hellman seemed to see a moral equivalence in their lives. She tried to talk to Orlova about the McCarthy period, "which had changed my life. . . . but that was tough going with a foreigner . . . and so I gave up, saying finally that I guessed you could survive if you felt like it, but you only knew that after you had survived."[8]

Hellman spent an evening with Orlova and Kopelev and their friends. There was talk of Kopelev's protest against wartime Red Army atrocities, which Hellman found "odd for a Jew who fought with the Russian armies all the way to Berlin," and so she told the company a little story that had been passed on to her by Averell Harriman: It seemed that in 1945, when Harriman had relayed Roosevelt's request to Stalin that he order his soldiers in Germany to behave with decorum, "Stalin had laughed and said he would so instruct the Russian armies, but he didn't believe that men who had been fighting for years could be kept from rape and loot." Orlova's friends greeted Hellman's anecdote with silence. It occurred to Hellman then, perhaps for the first time, that "Stalin is not a good man to quote these days."[9]

In June 1967, soon after Hellman returned from the Soviet Union, Dorothy Parker died. Hellman and Parker had been friends for some thirty years. Theirs had been an important friendship. They had laughed together, traveled together, been drunk together; they had liked and mocked the same people, were often guests at the same parties, guests at each other's houses. Hellman had disliked Parker's husband, and Hammett may have disliked Parker, but these antagonisms did not interfere with the friendship. Nothing came between them until Parker, twelve years older than Hellman, sank into decrepit old age, a lonely widow, out of the literary limelight, without money, and often drunk. Then Hellman pulled away.

Hellman is frank about her distaste for Parker at this stage of her life. She writes that she "did not want the burdens that Dottie, maybe by never asking for anything, always put on her friends. I was tired of trouble and wanted to be around people who walked faster than I and might pull me along with them. . . . And so, for the next five years of her life, I was not the good friend I had been. True, I was there in emergencies, but I was out the door immediately they were over."[10]

The emergencies were usually financial—Parker's medical bills, or the rent on her small apartment at the Volney Hotel, maybe even veterinarian bills for her poodle, Troy. Hellman was one of several friends called upon to supply the money needed, and when asked, she did, for old time's sake, and not without some expectation of return. There was, apparently, some understanding, or misunderstanding, between Hellman and Parker. Hellman assumed that she would be named as Parker's literary executor and have lifetime rights to Parker's copyrights.[11]

Parker did name Hellman as her literary executor, but she left her copyrights and royalties to Martin Luther King, Jr., along with what money she had, about $20,000. At King's death, everything was to pass to the NAACP. A year after Parker's death, King was assassinated. Contrary to Hellman's belief, the NAACP believed Parker's copyrights belonged to the organization. The dispute went to court, and in 1972 the court ruled against Hellman.

During the few years when she controlled Parker's work, Hellman, as she had with Hammett and his writings, thwarted Parker's potential biographers, and refused requests to quote from Parker's work. If Parker had left any papers, they were never found.[12]

"That goddamn bitch Dorothy Parker," Hellman said to her friend, the playwright Howard Teichmann. "I paid her hotel bill at the Volney for years, kept her in booze . . . all on the promise that when she died, she would leave me the rights to her writing."[13] A few years later Hellman explained to an interviewer that she had contested the NAACP to save her friend from her own worst impulses. Parker's understanding of black people had been incorrect: "It's one thing," Hellman said to Nora Ephron, "to have real feeling for black people, but to have the kind of blind sentimentality about the NAACP, a group so conservative that even many blacks now don't have any respect for it, is something else. [Parker] must have been drunk when she did it . . . Poor Dottie."[14] Nor did Hellman think much of Martin Luther King, Jr., who seemed to her just another of the "many Negro preachers from my childhood."[15]

By the late 1960s Hellman's political world view was out of fashion, viewed by a new generation as quaint, at best. But she was far from ready to be irrelevant. She had lived much of her life in public view, and much of her fame depended on her moral authority. In 1970 she organized the Committee for Public Justice, an organization designed to voice concern about a new period of political repression. At a news conference announcing the CPJ, Hellman said that "some of us thought we heard the voice of Joe McCarthy coming from the grave."[16]

The Committee denounced FBI abuses, investigated prison conditions, gave gala benefits to raise money, and published a newsletter called *Justice Department Watch*. For a decade Hellman was at the center of the Committee, enlisting new members, running meetings, raising funds, organizing events. The Committee did valuable work. With the star power of famous members, it was able to bring publicity to abuses of power under the Nixon Administration and to sponsor legislation. But for all her good work, Hellman was also a polarizing force on the Committee. Dorothy Samuels, for a time the executive director of the Committee, began making notes of Hellman's remarks at meetings, so that she could not later deny what she had said: "She was always making dramas out of nothing," Samuels said. "She would take things people had said and twist them around until they became dramas of some sort."[17] People who couldn't deal with the quarrels Hellman initiated—her rudeness to members and staff, especially to the younger women; her whimsical changes in policy direction; her baseless accusations of disloyalty, of lying, even of spying—quit. But Hellman kept the Committee in existence for more than ten years, until what energy remained to her was absorbed by her lawsuit against Mary McCarthy.

Hellman's almost life-long physical and mental energy was a gift from whatever good fairy attended her birth. She had done the hard work of running Hardscrabble Farm, had managed staff at her houses, had traveled and entertained extensively, had maintained an elaborate social and sexual life. She had written twelve plays and was fully involved in their production; she produced three volumes of memoirs. Finally, however, she was not immune from the effects of age and excess. The three or four packs of cigarettes Hellman had smoked daily for most of her life affected her heart and lungs. She drank, often more than was good for her. She began to have frequent falls, which may have been the consequence of small strokes—transient ischemic attacks. When she was sixty-nine, a small stroke was diagnosed, and it seems likely that more followed. TIAs are known to cause brain damage which often lead to personality changes and mood swings. In Hellman's case, friends noticed an intensification of her characteristic irritability and anger.[18] Enraged, she might now physically strike out with her umbrella or cane.[19] In the late 1970s, she developed glaucoma, which, in time, virtually blinded her. She saw a number of different doctors who prescribed medications that proved to be incompatible. In 1979, she spent a month in the hospital being detoxified. She had a pacemaker installed in 1981.

Peter Feibleman, Hellman's closest companion in her last years, noticed something more: "Some kind of change is going on in Lilly. Don't know what. Something about the way she walks and turns her head and the rhythm of her speech sometimes. . . . Something's screwing up her judgement. Feels as if a gear had slipped inside and she was reaching out for help." This was in 1976, the year *Scoundrel Time* was published.[20]

By 1979, anyone looking for signs of a problem with Hellman's mental state might have found it in the disjointed commentary Hellman wrote to accompany the republication of "Julia," in *Three:*

> I had expected to hear from Anne-Marie. But that has not happened, although last year a friend told me that Anne-Marie says she never really knew Julia, but that I was in love with her husband when we were all so very, very young. . . . I had a letter from a Dr. Smith, as I will name him here. He said he had been born in the house to which the wounded or already dead Julia had been brought, that his father was still living and why had I wanted to involve his father by claiming that he had issued a false death certificate? . . . Then Dr. Smith said his father had forbidden him to come to see me because of the younger Smith's "attitude." . . . I looked him up in the present London phone directory and no such name was listed as a doctor, although I guess he could be a research man in an institute. [21]

In 1980, Hellman published a small book called *Maybe*, which she calls a "story," although the narrator is named Lillian Hellman, and a man named Dashiell Hammett wanders through it. Some critics thought it was "a remarkable, intricate story . . . as carefully put together as a poem."[22] Others, that it was a book "about the erosion of certainty and the unknowability of truth."[23]

Maybe is certainly a strange book, which Hellman should have been saved from publishing, for it is so consistently confusing that the reader wonders whether it is Lillian Hellman the narrator, who is exploring the uncertainty of memory and the unknowability of truth, or Lillian Hellman the author, who is confused, and not in control of her own story:

> Certainly I know the so-called details of the story, but I am no longer sure whether all of them came from Sarah herself. I don't know how much was mishmash as told me, or if I half forgot and didn't even get it straight in the first place.[24]

Peter Feibleman speaks of *Maybe*'s creation as "a book written under the harshest kind of circumstances since an hour a day was the most [Hellman] could use her eyes."[25] Blindness and lack of mental focus certainly contributed to the problems of *Maybe*. Everything that was once solid for Hellman—her tight grip on her prose, on her characters, on her narrative— was slipping from her grasp. She must have felt it, but she could no more stop writing than she could stop smoking, and both activities, so defining to her life, had turned deadly:

"The kindest interpretation one can put on 'Maybe,'" Anatole Broyard wrote in the *New York Times*, . . . "is that it is a parody of contemporary fiction. . . . It is anybody's guess why Miss Hellman wrote 'Maybe.' It isn't fiction and as a memoir it reads like a disjointed hangover that lasted 40 years."[26]

15

---◆·◆·◆---

Mere Facts

"WHAT A word is truth," Lillian Hellman wrote in her introduction to her collected memoirs, "Slippery, tricky, unreliable. I tried in these books to tell the truth. I did not fool with facts. But, of course, that is a shallow definition of the truth." She told her students much the same sort of thing—that "truth is larger than the truth of fact."[1]

Despite Hellman's assurance that she did not fool with facts, she did seem to think them secondary matters, *mere* facts, rather than hard facts, cold facts, stubborn, naked, brutal, inescapable facts. No doubt, for example, it *felt* true to her that she had been in wartime Russia for six months rather than ten weeks; it also happened to strengthen her argument, and so she used the higher figure in writing a piece for the *New York Times*.[2] What seems most peculiar in Hellman's casual misuse of factual truth is her comfort with what might be so easily shown to be untrue.

In October 1979, Mary McCarthy appeared on the Dick Cavett show to promote her new novel *Cannibals and Missionaries*. In answer to a question about overrated writers, McCarthy said that she could think of only one: "Lillian Hellman, who I think is terribly overrated, a bad writer, and a dishonest writer."

"What is dishonest about her?" Cavett asked.

"Everything . . . every word she writes is a lie, including 'and' and 'the.'"

The recorded program was not shown until the night of January, 24, 1980, when Hellman saw it. She later told Peter Feibleman that she had "laughed out loud" when she heard McCarthy's words, but it could not have been a laugh of amusement for the next morning she called Ephraim London, her lawyer and her colleague on the Committee for Public Justice, and told him to sue McCarthy, Dick Cavett, and Channel Thirteen for $2,225,000. She claimed defamation: McCarthy had made a statement about her that was "false, made with ill-will, with malice, with knowledge of its falsity, with careless disregard of its truth, and with the intent to injure the plaintiff personally and professionally."

"I can't let Mary's poisonous nonsense go without taking a stand, can I?" she said to Feibleman. Feibleman was one of her friends who thought she should do that very thing.[3]

Mary McCarthy was not casual with facts: "What often seems to be at stake in Mary's writing and in her way of looking at things is a somewhat obsessional concern for the integrity of sheer fact in matters both trivial and striking," her friend Elizabeth Hardwick wrote.[4] McCarthy, herself, was explicit about what she expected from writing, and not just non-fiction: "If we read a novel, say, about conditions in postwar Germany, we expect it to be an accurate report of conditions in postwar Germany; if we find out that it is not, the novel is discredited . . . if Tolstoy was all wrong about the Battle of Borodino or the character of Napoleon, *War and Peace* would suffer."[5] Nor did she think that truth was slippery or unreliable: "Yes," she told Elizabeth Sifton who interviewed her for the *Paris Review*, "I believe there is a truth and that it's knowable."[6]

"Mary McCarthy's dislike for Lillian Hellman sprang . . . from the very center of her being," one of McCarthy's biographers wrote.[7] McCarthy put it more bluntly to an interviewer in 1978: "I can't stand her."[8]

As McCarthy recalled, she and Hellman first met in 1937, at a dinner party given by her then lover, Robert Misch.[9] Hellman was thirty-two, already famous for her Broadway hit *The Children's Hour.* She was a public supporter of the Moscow Trials, and she had recently returned from her visit to the war in Spain. McCarthy was twenty-five, and strikingly attractive, a fact which would not have been lost on Hellman. McCarthy was not yet famous as a writer, but she had a reputation in New York as a witty, fiercely opinionated reviewer of books and plays. She had recently joined the Committee for the Defense of Leon Trotsky. In McCarthy's recollection, she and Hellman had no conversation that night.

Their next meeting did not take place until a decade later, in 1948, at Sarah Lawrence, where McCarthy was teaching, and where Hellman had been invited to visit. This time they spoke. According to McCarthy, she arrived at a gathering in time to hear Hellman telling the students that John Dos Passos's break with the Loyalist side in the Spanish Civil War had to do with his dislike of the food in Madrid. McCarthy knew otherwise: While Dos Passos had been in Madrid he had learned that his old friend, Jose Robles, had been murdered by the Soviet advisors in Spain, who were eliminating dissenters to their control of the war. Hellman, McCarthy said, "was just brain-washing those girls—it was really vicious. So I finally spoke up and said, I'll tell you why he broke with the Loyalists." Hellman, McCarthy said, "trembled with rage."[10]

McCarthy, who often reviewed plays, seldom mentioned Hellman's name in print. She had seen *The Children's Hour* in 1934, and had liked it, but she did not write about the play. In a later review she had referred to the "oily virtuosity" of certain playwrights, and did mention Hellman's name among several others. She had not liked the adaptation of *Candide*, and had said so in print in 1957, but did not mention Hellman's name as the play's adaptor. Also in 1957, McCarthy wrote an article praising Arthur Miller for the bravery of his testimony before HUAC, and this piece must have cut close to Hellman's bone: "Called before the [Committee] last June, Mr. Miller declined to name the names of persons he had seen at Communist-sponsored meetings, although he testified freely about his own past association with Communist-front groups. . . . He was almost the only prominent figure heard by the Committee who did not either tell all or take refuge in the Fifth Amendment. . . . Against the ritual reply droned out so often during these past years—'I decline to answer on the ground that it might tend to incriminate me'—Mr. Miller's forthrightness struck a note of decided nonconformity." Without mentioning Hellman's name, McCarthy dismissed her cherished claim to uniqueness among HUAC's witnesses.[11]

For her part, Hellman seems to have publicly spoken disparagingly of McCarthy only once. In an interview with the *Paris Review* in 1964, she was asked about McCarthy's opinion of her work—that it was "too facile, relying on contrivance." Hellman answered: "I don't like to defend myself against Miss McCarthy's opinions, or anybody else's. I think Miss McCarthy is often brilliant and sometimes even sound. But, in fiction, she is . . . a lady magazine writer. Of course that doesn't mean she isn't right about me. But if I thought she was I'd quit."[12]

Although they seldom met, Hellman and McCarthy lived in overlapping worlds, and knew many of the same people; each was bound to hear news of the other. Both were writers after all, and aware of each other as such. McCarthy's first book of linked stories, *The Company She Keeps*, was a critical success and made her name. By the measure of money and reknown, Hellman was the more successful writer. But she was not necessarily admired by McCarthy's friends who were at the center of New York intellectual and literary life—Hannah Arendt, Philip Rahv, Dwight MacDonald, Robert Silvers—people whose friendship Hellman sought, but among whom she never gained complete acceptance or intimacy.

Of McCarthy's fiction, her novel *The Group*, based on her student years at Vassar, was most commercially, if not critically, successful. But her considerable reputation as an intellectual was based on her essays on literature and politics that appeared in the *New Yorker*, *Partisan Review*, *New York Review of Books*, *New Republic*—journals and magazines which, as Meyer Schapiro, the art historian and critic, said, "stood for perhaps a more accomplished style of writing and a more knowing audience than [Hellman] achieved."[13]

McCarthy began to write her memoirs while she was still in her forties. *Memories of a Catholic Girlhood* appeared in 1957 to a stunning review in the *New York Times*: "One of the most stinging, brilliant and disturbing memoirs ever written by an American. The autobiographical stories are marinated in italic commentaries that tell how much commonplace veracity or creative mendacity they contain . . . And probably the sharpest criticism of her [own] work you can find anywhere."[14]

Hellman's lawsuit against McCarthy in effect required McCarthy, a writer who loved facts, to review Hellman's memoirs. In a letter to her lawyer Ben O'Sullivan, McCarthy attempted to distinguish between the false statements in Hellman's memoirs, those "false in all respects, and [those] instances of intellectual dishonesty, which without outright lying amount to misrepresentation of the truth, often through concealment or through variations of the smear technique . . . The fact that she does not *say* in so many words . . . makes it a worse lie, because more specious and evasive than a lie direct. There are many examples of this kind of misrepresentation strewn through her 'autobiographies.' Indeed the peculiar effect of untruthfulness created by what she writes is that there is so little, often, that can be pinned down and refuted while so much, at the same time is insinuated."[15]

Of Hellman's three volumes of memoirs, McCarthy was particularly incensed by the most recent, *Scoundrel Time*, which "distort[s] events which are part of the plaintiff's time, distort and aggrandize her relationship to these events and are harshly unfair to many individuals, a few of whom are still living (or were at the time of publication) but most of whom are dead and unable to defend themselves."[16]

When news of the lawsuit broke, Hellman's friends took sides, not always hers. Norman Mailer went so far as to take out an ad in the magazine of the Sunday *New York Times*, pleading with both women to back off; Hellman ended her friendship with Mailer. William Styron mildly characterized the lawsuit to a reporter as "unfortunate"; Hellman wrote him a stinging letter of rebuke, to which he replied with a long letter of appeasement and protestations of his regard for her. It was true, Styron wrote, that he wished Hellman had done nothing in the face of McCarthy's attack; he thought silence much the best response to gratuitous insults. However, he assured Hellman of his "fondest love for you which, despite falterings and differences has never failed." It may say more about Styron than Hellman that he later wrote to his daughter, Susanna, in a different vein: "Miss Hellman, I fear, is utterly insane and loathsome to everyone, but is mercifully immobilized by her cigarette, her blindness, feebleness and venom and so can really bite no one seriously."[17]

"Lillian," Joseph Rauh said to her on the telephone, "every one of us has told a fib now and then. If this ever got to court, they could bring up every word you ever wrote or said and examine it for truthfulness. Do you really want that?" Hellman hung up in a rage.[18] Hellman's friend Dr. Milton Wexler told her directly that she would lose the case; she replied: "I'm going to destroy that bitch. I'm going to prove that she's stupid, I'm going to prove that she doesn't know how to write, that nobody should respect her."[19]

The lawsuit dragged on for more than three years. At one point Ephraim London asked Ben O'Sullivan to lunch. London suggested that if McCarthy would publicly apologize for her remarks, Hellman might withdraw the lawsuit. McCarthy refused. Her position was that she had spoken the truth and she wanted to face Hellman in court.

And all the while McCarthy was gathering evidence, reading Hellman's work closely, asking everyone who knew anything about Hellman's life to help her. "People came out of the woodwork to corroborate Mary's experience. . . . Mary was just alight with excitement. She was hot on the trail . . . She loved every minute of it."[20]

Martha Gellhorn, whose distaste for Hellman dated to 1937 and their shipboard meeting en route to France, wrote an article for the *Paris Review* casting an eyewitness's doubt on almost every aspect of Hellman's account of her experiences in Spain.[21] Through Stephen Spender, who had been a friend of Muriel Gardiner's since the 1930s, McCarthy learned about "Julia," the one Hellman story that was not amorphous but full of extraordinarily specific details that might prove to be "the lie direct." "Lizzie [Hardwick] has had a very sharp, indeed brilliant thought about 'Julia,'" McCarthy wrote to her lawyer. "If the story was *true*, what made Hellman change the names. Nobody could have been hurt . . . it could only have redounded to the dead friend's credit to have the story told and her name honored. In fact it was H's *duty* to proclaim 'Julia's' heroism."[22]

In the late 1960s, or early seventies, in any case shortly before she wrote the Julia story, Hellman had tried it out on a number of people. One day, at lunch, she told Norman Podhoretz that she was in a quandary; there had been an incident in her life, she said, which she had promised to keep secret, but now she felt impelled to write about it. Podhoretz heard her out and failed to see why the story should be kept secret.

"So you think it would be okay if I wrote about it?" Hellman asked him. Podhoretz assured her that he saw no reason not to.[23]

Peter Feibleman, too, had been told the story of Hellman's girlhood friend who had been killed resisting the Nazis. Feibleman was staying with Hellman on the Vineyard as she wrote the story; she showed him pages as she went along, figuring out the details with him—what sort of wallpaper might have hung in a Berlin cafe in the 1930s? What would the entrance to the funeral parlor have looked like? Which ship might she have taken to bring Julia's body back to the States? "Because I was interested in what she was doing," Feibleman wrote, "it never occurred to me at the time that people would take all the details of the story for literal truth, since it seemed so clear that she was fusing fact and fiction."[24]

Podhoretz, who had believed the story when Hellman told it to him over lunch, read "Julia" when it was published in *Pentimento* in 1973 and found it incredible: "The story as she had told it seemed genuine enough, but on paper it came out sounding as false as everything else she had written in the same Hemingway-via-Hammett prose style."[25] Reviewing *Pentimento*, Clive James, the Australian critic, also felt a pervasive tone of falsity: "For the truth is that the Julia chapter, like all the others, happens in a dream . . . the story reads like a spy-sketch by Nichols and May . . . To have been there, to have seen it, and yet still be able to write it down so that it rings false—it takes a special kind of talent."[26]

Hellman's confidence in "Julia" had not been shaken by a few negative reviews. Muriel Gardiner's letter to her, dated October 1976, may have given her some pause, but Hellman had decided to ignore the letter. And for a number of years, as she heard nothing more from Gardiner, and no one else came forward to challenge the story, Hellman doubled down on her claim to Julia, repeating to an interviewer what she had written in the story: "But nothing on God's earth could have shaken my memory about [Julia.] I did finally look at whatever notes I had left, but I didn't need to."[27]

Not long before the movie of "Julia" was released in 1977, Hellman posed for an advertisement for Blackglama mink. A full page photograph of herself swathed in fur, seemingly naked underneath, holding a lit cigarette, appeared in national women's magazines. It was one of a series of such advertisements—*What Becomes a Legend Most*—that included women, most of them movie stars, so famous they did not need to be named. Hellman's face was as famous as any. As famous as Jane Fonda's, who played Lillian in the movie of Julia, or Vanessa Redgrave's who played Julia. *Julia* was released without incident in 1977. It won three Oscars. Hellman's triumph seemed unchallengeable, and she went on to other things. She worked on the comments she was adding to the edition of her collected memoirs to be published under the title *Three*, in 1979. She wrote her novella, *Maybe*, which was published a year later.

But in the spring of 1983, as Hellman's suit against McCarthy slowly wound its way through the legal system, Muriel Gardiner was about to publish *Code Name Mary*, her own account of her experiences in the Austrian underground. In the introduction to her book Gardiner wrote that she had been "struck by the many similarities between my life" and Hellman's character of Julia. And just as *Code Name Mary* was about to be released, the *New York Times* picked up on a possible literary scandal. The respected biographer Joseph Lash, who had written biographies of Eleanor and Franklin Roosevelt, had given Gardiner's book a cover blurb which seemed very pointed: "No self-styled thriller can match this book's story. There are no fantasies. Names are named. There are real Socialists and Communists as well as Nazis and Fascists. They are recognizable and verifiable."

In an interview with the *Times*, Lash was asked whether he had been thinking of Hellman's "Julia," when he wrote Gardiner's blurb. He admitted that he had been. "The thing that appalled me," Lash said, "was that 'Julia' ends up with Lillian Hellman bringing Julia's body back to this country. Well, if Julia is, in effect, Muriel Gardiner, then I think readers are entitled to some explanation."

The *Times* reported Hellman's response: "Miss Hellman said that she had never heard of Dr. Gardiner until this week. 'She may have been the model for somebody else's Julia, but she was certainly not the model for my Julia,' she said."

Had Gardiner written her a letter?

"Miss Hellman said if she received such a letter she doesn't remember it." Informed by the *Times* reporter that Gardiner had been given assurances by the director of the Austrian underground archives that she was the only American woman whose name was recorded in the archives of the resistance movement, Hellman responded: "Who would keep archives of an underground movement? That's comedy stuff. A real underground movement would have been in hiding and would have had almost no records."[28]

The chutzpah of Hellman's challenge is breathtaking: *she* knew better about the record-keeping habits of underground movements in the Nazi era than the director of its archives.

Cornered, she had held her ground. But in May, just as Gardiner's book was released, Hellman tried to arrange a meeting with Gardiner, hoping to persuade her to make a statement denying that she was Julia. Gardiner first agreed to see her, but she had learned enough about Hellman at that point to be wary, and the meeting never took place. At one point Gardiner received a telephone call from Hellman's analyst, Dr. George Gero; he asked whether she would make a statement to that effect that she was not Julia. Gardiner replied that she would have to "disappoint" Miss Hellman; since she had never claimed to be Julia, she could not claim not to be.[29]

And now, Hellman's loyal lawyer, Ephraim London, was pleading with Hellman for Julia's real name. Hellman flailed. At lunch with London and Blair Clark, she came up with a name, but it was soon clear that she had pulled it out of thin air. She then said that she had received a threatening letter from a lawyer named "Wolf" telling her that Julia's family would sue her for defaming them if she named them.

Where was this letter?

Hellman couldn't find it.

How could it be that Julia's parents were still alive? Hellman was in her late seventies; hadn't she and Julia been girl-hood friends?

Oh, no, Hellman suddenly remembered; Julia was actually ten years younger than she was.[30]

For so many years Hellman had cultivated and, for the most part, achieved a reputation as a woman of moral courage, honesty, and integrity. The McCarthy suit, if it came to court, would bring down the edifice of her life. Did she not understand how vulnerable she was? McCarthy speculated that Hellman was so convinced of her own rectitude, so "persuaded . . . of her version of the truth," that she was "deaf to any other."[31] Sid Perelman, Hellman's friend of more than forty years, had written to a mutual friend of theirs in 1974: "I'm in a cold rage at La Hellman . . . people have been feeding her vanity to the point where it's becoming insufferable . . . the compliments that she's forced out of us to buttress her self-esteem . . . the phone calls from her publishers congratulating her, and all that sort of rot piled upon the hosannas about [*An Unfinished Woman*] have puffed her ego out of all recognition."[32]

It was no secret to Hellman's friends that she "didn't know the boundary between fact and fiction," as Norman Mailer said after Hellman's death.[33] In her personal life this would matter only to her friends; they could take her with a grain of salt, or not at all. But Hellman had a public life, and she wrote about it. She wrote about herself as witness to the world—in Moscow, in Spain, in Vienna and Berlin, in Finland, in Washington, at the very time of crucial historical events. Her readers saw the world through her eyes. She wrote about her relations with celebrated people—Hammett, Hemingway, Dorothy Parker, Scott Fitzgerald—and her readers saw them through her often unadmiring eyes. Does it matter if she was actually in all those places, at those times, and if she saw what she said she did? Does it matter if the tales she tells about other writers are true? Does it matter if one or many of the stories that make up her memoirs are invented? Readers enjoyed them and, after all, every memoirist, everyone who tries to tell a true story for that matter, fails in some degree. It is not truth that is tricky and unreliable, as Hellman would have it. Memory is the problem: the color of a dress, the arrangement of furniture in a room, the words of a conversation—these things can be lost or confused. Truth remains in the facts; facts can be verified, but only if the writer cares to do so.

Hellman either knew or did not know a Julia. Stalin did or did not offer Hellman an interview. A voice from the balcony of the HUAC hearing room did or did not call out to congratulate her for her guts. Hemingway did or did not suggest that she join him on the balcony in Spain to watch the beauty of the falling bombs. She did or did not belong to the Communist Party.

A few years ago the historian and author Timothy Garton Ash, whose subject is Central and Eastern Europe, wrote with strong feeling about what he called the "frontier" between the "literature of fact" and the "literature of fiction":

> Imagination is the sun that illuminates both countries. But this leads us into temptation. A voice in your ear whispers . . . "look, just across the frontier there is that gorgeous flower—the one missing novelistic detail that will bring the whole story alive. Pop across and pick it. No one will notice." I know this voice, I have heard it. But if we claim to write the literature of fact, it must be resisted.
>
> Why? For moral reasons, above all. Words written about the real world have consequences in the real world . . . moral reasons are sufficient; but there are artistic ones too. Writers often cross this frontier because they think their work will be enhanced as a result. Reportage or history will become Literature. Paragraph for paragraph that may be true. But as a whole, the work is diminished.[34]

Hellman might have called her stories fiction and been judged on literary merit alone. Instead, she promised that she had not fooled with the facts of her life, all the while crossing and re-crossing the frontier without a by-your-leave. Like the man who comes courting without mentioning the wife and children at home, she wanted something for nothing.

How can it *not* matter that Hellman refused the distinction between fact and fiction, when facts are life's North Star? It is the one question we always ask of those who bring us news of the world: Did that *really* happen? Is that *true?*

Hellman spent the last winter of her life, 1983–1984, in Los Angeles, where she lived in the house of Talli Wyler, the widow of her friend, the director, William Wyler. Hellman was very ill and very frail that winter. She had to be carried up and down the flight of stairs leading to her rooms at Wyler's house. She needed round-the-clock nurses, at whom her temper often exploded. Still, with the help of nurses and friends, and a wheelchair, she often went out to dinner. In the spring, Hellman returned to New York, and then, with nurses, to her beachfront house on Martha's Vineyard.

In early June, less than a month before she died, Hellman suffered another blow to her reputation. An article entitled "Julia and Other Fictions by Lillian Hellman," commissioned by Hellman's former friend Norman Podhoretz, appeared in *Commentary* magazine. The author of the piece, Samuel McCracken, applied himself with great attention to the details of Hellman's memoirs, particularly those in "Julia." He checked French timetables, ship schedules, locations of funeral homes in London. Was it possible that Hellman had traveled from Paris to Berlin to Moscow in 1937 in the way she said she did? Did the ship on which Hellman said she brought Julia's body from London to the United States in 1938 actually make port in England? McCracken checked what could be checked in the chronology of Hellman's travels, and he concluded that what she had written was at best implausible, at worst impossible. In short, McCracken showed that many of the details Hellman offered as fact, collapsed on scrutiny; on a literary level, they were so implausible they would have disgraced "a third-rate thriller."

Hellman, blind, had the McCracken piece read to her. How would she have dealt with this final assault on her honor had she but strength enough and time? She was out of both. She died in the early morning hours of the last day of June, with only a nurse to hear her last breath. Her lawsuit against McCarthy died with her.

Hellman's death was a disappointment to McCarthy who

would have dearly liked to face Hellman in court. And maybe Hellman wanted that too, believing that she could prevail against legal arguments in court just as she prevailed at her own dinner table, just as she did in life, ending arguments disagreeable to her with a haughty, "Forgive me, but . . ." She was Lillian Hellman, after all.

NOTES

Prologue

1. Deborah Martinson, *Lillian Hellman: A Life with Foxes and Scoundrels* (Berkeley: Counterpoint Press, 2005), 356.

2. Carol Brightman, *Writing Dangerously: Mary McCarthy and Her World* (New York: Clarkson Potter, 1992), 611.

3. Lillian Hellman, *Three: An Unfinished Woman, Pentimento, Scoundrel Time* (Boston: Little, Brown, 1979), 258.

4. Hellman, *Three*, 30–39.

Chapter 1. The Hubbards of Bowden

1. Eric Bentley, *In Search of Theater* (New York: Vintage, 1954), 9.

2. Elizabeth Hardwick, "The Little Foxes Revived," *The New York Review of Books*, December 21, 1967.

Chapter 2. The Marxes of Demopolis

Much of the material about the Marx family, and about Jewish life in Demopolis, Alabama, is based on research by Alan Goodman Koch, an independent scholar. Mr. Koch generously shared his documentary material with me, and discussed his knowledge of this area in which he was raised. He and his wife, Linda, also took me to Demopolis and served as my guides to the town and its residents.

1. Hasia R. Diner, *The Jews of the United States: 1654–2000* (Berkeley: University of California Press, 2006), passim.

2. Jonathan D. Sarna, "American Judaism," collected in *From Haven to Home: 350 Years of Jewish Life in America*, ed. Michael W. Grunberger (New York: George Braziller for the Library of Congress, 2004), passim.

3. Diner, *Jews of the United States*.

4. Winston Smith, *The People's City: The Glory and Grief of an Alabama Town, 1850–1874* (Demopolis, Alabama: Marengo County Historical Society, 2003), Epigraph to Part One: An Antebellum Society, 1850–1860.

5. "Visualizing Slavery," county map of 1861, *New York Times*, published December 10, 2010.

6. Lillian Hellman, *Three: An Unfinished Woman, Pentimento, Scoundrel Time* (Boston: Little, Brown, 1979), 15.

7. Hellman, *Three*, 14–15.

8. Jerry Z. Muller, *Capitalism and the Jews* (Princeton, N.J.: Princeton University Press, 2010), 84.

9. Thomas McAdory Owen and Marie Bankhead Owen, *History of Alabama and Dictionary of Alabama Biography*, Vol. 4 (Chicago: S. J. Clarke Publishing Company, 1921), 1171.

10. The United States Census of 1860; Smith, *The People's City*, 11–14.

11. Robert Warshow, *The Immediate Experience: Movies, Comics, Theatre, and Other Aspects of Popular Culture* (New York: Atheneum, 1962), review of Sholem Aleichem, 266.

12. Robert Rosen, "Jewish Confederates," in *Jewish Roots in Southern Soil: A New History*, ed. Marcie Ferris and Mark I. Greenberg (Waltham, MA: Brandeis University Press), 110.

13. Rosen, "Jewish Confederates," 113.

14. Rosen, "Jewish Confederates," 109, 118.

15. Charles S. Watson, *The History of Southern Drama* (Lexington: University Press of Kentucky, 1997).

16. Alabama Civil War Database, Alabama Department of Archives and History.

17. Owen and Owen, *History of Alabama*, 1171; also 1870 Census.

18. Historic American Building Survey, Archeology and Historic Preservation, National Park Service, Department of the Interior, Washington, D.C.

19. Smith, *The People's City*, 237.

20. Owen and Owen, *History of Alabama*, 1171.

21. Deborah Martinson, *Lillian Hellman: A Life with Foxes and Scoundrels* (Berkeley: Counterpoint Press, 2005), 29.

Chapter 3. Two Jewish Girls

1. Brenda Wineapple, *Sister Brother: Gertrude and Leo Stein* (New York: G. P. Putnam's Sons, 1996). See also Janet Malcolm, *Two Lives: Gertrude and Alice* (New Haven: Yale University Press, 2007), 35.

2. Jackson R. Bryer, ed., *Conversations with Lillian Hellman* (Jackson: University Press of Mississippi, 1986), 63; William Wright, *Lillian Hellman: The Image, the Woman* (New York: Simon and Schuster, 1986), 106–7.

3. Hemingway quoted in Michael S. Reynolds, *Hemingway: The Final Years* (New York: W. W. Norton, 2000), 173. See also Malcolm, *Two Lives*.

4. Lillian Hellman, *Three: An Unfinished Woman, Pentimento, Scoundrel Time* (Boston: Little, Brown, 1979), 90.

5. Joan Mellen, *Hellman and Hammett: The Legendary Passion of Lillian Hellman and Dashiell Hammett* (New York: HarperPerennial, 1997), 127.

6. Wineapple, *Sister Brother*, 14.

7. Elizabeth Hardwick, *American Fictions* (New York: Modern Library, 1999), 92–93.

8. Malcolm, *Two Lives*, 27–28.

9. Mellen, *Hellman and Hammett*, 12.

10. Malcolm, *Two Lives*, 79.

11. *New York Times*, May 6, 1934; *The Journal of Historical Review*, September–October 1977, p. 22.

12. Robert Warshow, "Gerty and the G.I.'s" in *The Immediate Experience: Movies, Comics, Theatre, and Other Aspects of Popular Culture* (New York: Atheneum, 1962), 281.

13. James Laughlin, *The Way It Wasn't: From the Files of James Laughlin* (New York: New Directions, 2006), 90.

14. Malcolm, *Two Lives*, passim.

15. Maurice Grosser, "Gertrude Stein and Alice Toklas," in *The Company They Kept: Writers and Their Unforgettable Friendships*, ed. Robert B. Silvers and Barbara Epstein (New York: New York Review of Books, 2006), 159.

16. Quoted from Mellen, *Hellman and Hammett*, 142.

17. Carl E. Rollyson, *Lillian Hellman: Her Legend and Her Legacy* (New York: St. Martin's Press, 1988), 415.

18. Rollyson, *Lillian Hellman*, 413.

19. Sylvie Drake, in Bryer, ed., *Conversations with Lillian Hellman*, 291.

20. Lillian Hellman, *The Collected Plays* (Boston: Little, Brown, 1972), 239 (emphasis added).

21. Mellen, *Hellman and Hammett*, 172.

Chapter 4. Marriage

1. Deborah Martinson, *Lillian Hellman: A Life with Foxes and Scoundrels* (Berkeley: Counterpoint Press, 2005), 40–42.

2. Lillian Hellman, *Three: An Unfinished Woman, Pentimento, Scoundrel Time* (Boston: Little, Brown, 1979), 54.

3. Hellman, *Three*, 6.

4. Carl E. Rollyson, *Lillian Hellman: Her Legend and Her Legacy* (New York: St. Martin's Press, 1988), 47.

5. Hellman, *Three*, 64.

6. Joan Mellen, *Hellman and Hammett: The Legendary Passion of Lillian Hellman and Dashiell Hammett* (New York: HarperPerennial, 1997), 17.

7. Martinson, *Lillian Hellman*, 79.

8. Martinson, *Lillian Hellman*, 54.

9. Rollyson, *Lillian Hellman*, 167.

10. Mellen, *Hellman and Hammett*, 16.

11. "Arthur Kober: No Regella Yankee," Wendell Howard, Polish American Historical Association newsletter, Vol. 40, No. 1, Spring 1993.

12. Mellen, *Hellman and Hammett*, 36.

13. Hellman, *Three*, 62–63.

14. Diane Johnson, *The Life of Dashiell Hammett* (London: Picador, 1985), 13–14.

15. Johnson, *Dashiell Hammett*, 13.

16. Dashiell Hammett, *Selected Letters of Dashiell Hammett*, ed. Richard Layman and Julie Rivett (Washington, DC: Counterpoint, 2001).

17. Johnson, *Dashiell Hammett*, 56–57.

18. Johnson, *Dashiell Hammett*, 87.

19. Johnson, *Dashiell Hammett*, 57.

20. Johnson, *Dashiell Hammett*, 78.

21. Mellen, *Hellman and Hammett*, 34.

22. Johnson, *Dashiell Hammett*, 96.

23. William Wright, *Lillian Hellman: The Image, the Woman* (New York: Simon and Schuster, 1986), 70.

24. Rollyson, *Lillian Hellman*, 97.

25. Mellen, *Hellman and Hammett*, 40.

26. F. Scott Fitzgerald, *The Beautiful and Damned* (Rockville, MD: Serenity Publishers, 2009), 207.

27. Mellen, *Hellman and Hammett*, from Kober's archive in Wisconsin, 49–50.

28. Martinson, *Lillian Hellman*, 82.

29. Mellen, *Hellman and Hammett*, 50.

Chapter 5. The Writing Life: 1933–1984

1. Diane Johnson, *Dashiell Hammett: A Life* (New York: Random House, 1983), 101–2.

2. Richard Layman and Julie Rivett, eds., *Selected Letters of Dashiell Hammett* (Washington, DC: Counterpoint, 2001).

3. Joan Mellen, *Hellman and Hammett: The Legendary Passion of Lillian Hellman and Dashiell Hammett* (New York: Harper-Perennial, 1997), 198.

4. Layman and Rivett, eds., *Selected Letters of Dashiell Hammett,* 277.

5. Deborah Martinson, *Lillian Hellman: A Life with Foxes and Scoundrels* (Berkeley: Counterpoint Press, 2005), 117.

6. Mellen, *Hellman and Hammett,* 124.

7. Jackson R. Bryer, ed., *Conversations with Lillian Hellman* (Jackson: University Press of Mississippi, 1986), 126.

8. Bryer, ed., *Conversations with Lillian Hellman,*13.

9. Lillian Hellman, *Three: An Unfinished Woman, Pentimento, Scoundrel Time* (Boston: Little, Brown, 1979), 454.

10. Hellman, *Three,* 472.

11. Hellman, *Three,* 474–75.

12. Hellman, *Three,* 495.

13. Bryer, ed., *Conversations with Lillian Hellman,* 9.

14. Peter S. Feibleman, *Lilly: Reminiscences of Lillian Hellman* (New York: Morrow, 1988), 33–34.

Chapter 6. Along Came a Spider

1. Lillian Hellman, *Three: An Unfinished Woman, Pentimento, Scoundrel Time* (Boston: Little, Brown, 1979), 91.

2. Hellman, *Three,* 205.

3. Robert Conquest, *The Great Terror: Stalin's Purge of the Thirties* (New York: Macmillan, 1968), 465.

4. Conquest, *The Great Terror,* 102.

5. Conquest, *The Great Terror,* 464.

6. I. F. Stone, *The War Years, 1939–1945* (Boston: Little, Brown, 1988), 4.

7. Peggy Dennis, *The Autobiography of an American Communist: A Personal View of a Political Life* (Westport, Conn.: Lawrence Hill, 1977).

8. *New Masses,* May 3, 1938.

9. Phyllis Jacobson, *New Politics,* Summer, 1997.

10. Hellman, *Three,* 92.

11. Michael Scammell, *Koestler: The Literary and Political Od-*

yssey of a Twentieth-Century Skeptic (New York: Random House, 2009), 105.

12. Deborah Martinson, *Lillian Hellman: A Life with Foxes and Scoundrels* (Berkeley: Counterpoint Press, 2005), 170.

13. Lillian Hellman papers, FBI, cited in Robert P. Newman, *The Cold War Romance of Lillian Hellman and John Melby* (Chapel Hill: University of North Carolina Press, 1989), 297.

14. Carl E. Rollyson, *Lillian Hellman: Her Legend and Her Legacy* (New York: St. Martin's Press, 1988), 432.

15. John Dos Passos, *The Theme Is Freedom* (New York: Dodd, Mead and Company, 1956), 115.

16. Elinor Langer, *Josephine Herbst* (Little, Brown, 1984), 233.

17. Hellman, *Three*, 98.

18. Tony Judt, *The New York Review of Books*, September 21, 2006.

19. Judt, quoting Leszek Kołakowski, *The New York Review of Books*, September 21, 2006.

20. Hellman, *Three*, 131–32.

21. Rollyson, *Lillian Hellman*, 91, ca. 1935.

22. Joan Mellen, *Hellman and Hammett: The Legendary Passion of Lillian Hellman and Dashiell Hammett* (New York: HarperPerennial, 1997), 113.

23. Kober diary, January, 7, 1938, quoted in Mellen, *Hellman and Hammett*, 128.

24. Hellman, *Three*, 203.

25. *The New Review*, May 1974.

26. Interview with Peter Feibleman, in Mellen, *Hellman and Hammett*, 371.

Chapter 7. Eros

1. Lillian Hellman, *Three: An Unfinished Woman, Pentimento, Scoundrel Time* (Boston: Little, Brown, 1979), 210.

2. Joan Mellen, *Hellman and Hammett: The Legendary Passion of Lillian Hellman and Dashiell Hammett* (New York: HarperPerennial, 1997), 365.

3. Mellen, *Hellman and Hammett*, 369.

4. Hellman, *Three*, 42, 45.

5. Hellman, *Three*, 151.

6. Hellman, *Three*, 383–84.

7. Hellman, *Three*, 48.

8. Mellen, *Hellman and Hammett*, 197.

9. Mellen, *Hellman and Hammett*, 253.

10. Diane Johnson, *Vanity Fair*, "Obsessed," May 1985.

11. Johnson, *Vanity Fair*, quoted in Mellen, *Hellman and Hammett*, 141.

12. Peter S. Feibleman, *Lilly: Reminiscences of Lillian Hellman* (New York: Morrow, 1988), 168.

13. Mellen, *Hellman and Hammett*, 154.

14. Robert P. Newman, *The Cold War Romance of Lillian Hellman and John Melby* (Chapel Hill: University of North Carolina Press, 1989), 38.

15. Mellen, *Hellman and Hammett*, 245.

16. Newman, *Cold War Romance*, 117, 112.

17. Newman, *Cold War Romance*, 122.

18. Newman, *Cold War Romance*, 175, 179, 215.

19. Diary quoted in Deborah Martinson, *Lillian Hellman: A Life with Foxes and Scoundrels* (Berkeley: Counterpoint Press, 2005), 232.

20. Martinson, *Lillian Hellman*, 232.

21. Elia Kazan, *Elia Kazan: A Life* (New York: Knopf, 1988), 441–42.

22. Kazan, *Elia Kazan*, 382.

23. Hellman, *Three*, 515.

24. Hellman, *Three*, 537.

25. Feibleman, *Lilly*, 53.

26. Feibleman, *Lilly*, 126.

27. Feibleman, *Lilly*, 143.

28. Feibleman, *Lilly*, 339.

Chapter 8. Counterparts

1. Mary McCarthy papers, Box 259, Vassar College Archives and Special Collections.

2. Carl E. Rollyson, *Lillian Hellman: Her Legend and Her Legacy* (New York: St. Martin's Press, 1988), 319, citing Joseph Rauh papers.

3. Muriel Gardiner, *Code Name Mary: Memoirs of an American Woman in the Austrian Underground* (New Haven: Yale University Press, 1983), 83–84.

4. Gardiner, *Code Name Mary*, 150.

5. Joan Mellen, *Hellman and Hammett: The Legendary Passion of Lillian Hellman and Dashiell Hammett* (New York: HarperPerennial, 1997), 172.

6. Mellen, *Hellman and Hammett*, 174.

7. Mellen, *Hellman and Hammett*, 169.

8. Lillian Hellman, *Three: An Unfinished Woman, Pentimento, Scoundrel Time* (Boston: Little, Brown, 1979), 114.

9. *Pravda*, December 17, 1936, cited by Dorothy Gallagher, *All the Right Enemies: The Life and Murder of Carlo Tresca* (New Brunswick, N.J.: Rutgers University Press, 1988), 153.

10. David Caute, *The Fellow Travellers: Intellectual Friends of Communism* (New Haven: Yale University Press, 1988), 142.

11. Jonathan Miles, *The Dangerous Otto Katz: The Many Lives of a Soviet Spy* (New York: Bloomsbury, 2010), 295; Heda Kovaly, *Under a Cruel Star: A Life in Prague* (Cambridge, Mass.: Plunkett Lake Press, 1986).

Chapter 9. The Incurious Tourist

1. Anne Applebaum, *Gulag: A History* (New York: Doubleday, 2003), 441.

2. William Wright, *Lillian Hellman: The Image, the Woman* (New York: Simon and Schuster, 1986), 198; Robert P. Newman, *The Cold War Romance of Lillian Hellman and John Melby* (Chapel Hill: University of North Carolina Press, 1989), 39.

3. Wright, *Lillian Hellman*, 197.

4. Lillian Hellman, *Three: An Unfinished Woman, Pentimento, Scoundrel Time* (Boston: Little, Brown, 1979), 164.

5. Joan Mellen, *Hellman and Hammett: The Legendary Passion of Lillian Hellman and Dashiell Hammett* (New York: HarperPerennial, 1997), 231.

6. Hellman, *Three*, 149–50.

7. Isaiah Berlin, "Pasternak and Akhmatova," in *The Company They Kept: Writers and Their Unforgettable Friendships*, ed. Robert B. Silvers and Barbara Epstein (New York: New York Review of Books, 2006), 70.

8. Nadezhda Mandelstam, *Hope Against Hope* (New York: Atheneum, 1970), 175.

9. Nina Nikolaevna Berberova, *The Italics Are Mine* (New York: Harcourt, Brace, and World, 1969), 140.

10. Hellman, *Three*, 150–51.

11. Carl E. Rollyson, *Lillian Hellman: Her Legend and Her Legacy* (New York: St. Martin's Press, 1988), 226.

12. Hellman, *Three*, 205.

13. George F. Kennan, *Memoirs* (Boston: Little, Brown, 1967), 210.

14. Tony Judt, *Postwar: A History of Europe since 1945* (New York: Penguin, 2005), 102.

15. Hellman, *Three*, 169.

16. Raisa Orlova, *Memoirs* (New York: Random House, 1983), 116.

17. Jackson R. Bryer, ed., *Conversations with Lillian Hellman* (Jackson: University Press of Mississippi, 1986), 174.

18. Hellman, *Three*, 284.

19. Hellman, *Three*, 284.

20. Hellman, *Three*, 183.

21. Alfred Kazin, *New York Jew* (New York: Knopf, 1978), 269.

Chapter 10. Lillian Hellman's Analyst

1. Dr. Mark Leffert, "The Psychoanalysis of George Gershwin: An American Tragedy," *Journal of the American Academy of Psychoanalysis and Dynamic Psychiatry*, 2011. Kay Swift from Katharine Weber, *The Memory of All That: George Gershwin, Kay Swift and My Family's Legacy of Infidelities* (New York: Crown Publishers, 2011), passim.

2. Lillian Hellman, *Three: An Unfinished Woman, Pentimento, Scoundrel Time* (Boston: Little, Brown, 1979), 226–27.

3. Peter S. Feibleman, *Lilly: Reminiscences of Lillian Hellman* (New York: Morrow, 1988), 218.

4. Joan Mellen, *Hellman and Hammett: The Legendary Passion of Lillian Hellman and Dashiell Hammett* (New York: HarperPerennial, 1997),143.

Chapter 11. "You Are What You Are to Me"

1. The chapter title is from a letter from Hammett to Hellman, January 14, 1958, quoted in Diane Johnson, *Dashiell Hammett: A Life* (New York: Random House, 1983), 290. Joan Mellen, *Hellman and Hammett: The Legendary Passion of Lillian Hellman and Dashiell Hammett* (New York: HarperPerennial, 1997), 286.

2. Mellen, *Hellman and Hammett*, 286.

3. Lillian Hellman, *Three: An Unfinished Woman, Pentimento, Scoundrel Time* (Boston: Little, Brown, 1979), 501.

4. Johnson, *Dashiell Hammett*, 245–47.

5. Diane Johnson, "Obsessed," *Vanity Fair*, May 1985.

6. Mellen, *Hellman and Hammett*, 287.

7. Jo Hammett, *Dashiell Hammett, A Daughter Remembers* (New York: Carroll and Graf, 2001), 151.

8. Richard Layman and Julie Rivett, eds., *Selected Letters of Dashiell Hammett* (Washington, DC: Counterpoint, 2001), April 10, 1952.

9. Alice Kessler-Harris, *A Difficult Woman: The Challenging Life and Times of Lillian Hellman* (New York: Bloomsbury, 2012), 61.

10. William Wright, *Lillian Hellman: The Image, the Woman* (New York: Simon and Schuster, 1986), 266.

11. Kessler-Harris, *A Difficult Woman*, quote from Hellman's appointment books, 209.

12. Hellman, *Scoundrel Time* (Boston: Little, Brown, 1976), 157.

13. Jo Hammett, *Dashiell Hammett*, 165–66.

14. Wright, *Lillian Hellman*, 297; Jo Hammett, *Dashiell Hammett*, 83.

15. Wright, *Lillian Hellman*, 297.

16. Mellen, *Hellman and Hammett*, 361–62.

17. Johnson, "Obsessed," *Vanity Fair*, May 1985.

18. Hammett, *Selected Letters*, January 17, 1958.

Chapter 12. Having Her Say

1. Lillian Hellman, *Three: An Unfinished Woman, Pentimento, Scoundrel Time* (Boston: Little, Brown, 1979), 726.

2. Hellman, *Scoundrel Time*, 42–43.

3. Hellman, *Three*, 726.

4. Hellman, *Scoundrel Time*, 43.

5. Tony Judt with Timothy Snyder, *Thinking the Twentieth Century* (New York: Penguin, 2012), 226.

6. Rauh papers, Truman Library, cited by Carl E. Rollyson, *Lillian Hellman: Her Legend and Her Legacy* (New York: St. Martin's Press, 1988), 319.

7. David Caute, *The Fellow Travellers: Intellectual Friends of Communism* (New Haven: Yale University Press, 1988), 314.

8. Murray Kempton, *Rebellions, Perversities and Main Events* (New York: Times Books, 1994), 110.

9. Michael Wrezin, *Interviews with Dwight MacDonald* (Jackson: University Press of Mississippi, 2003), 137–39.

10. Joseph Rauh, *Oral History*, 1989, Truman Library.

11. *New York Times*, May 22, 1952 (emphasis added).

12. Rollyson, *Lillian Hellman*, 318.

13. Rollyson, *Lillian Hellman*, 329, 330.

14. Quoted by Murray Kempton, *The New York Review of Books*, June 10, 1976.

15. Kempton, *New York Review of Books*, June 10, 1976.

16. Sidney Hook, *Encounter*, February 1977.

17. Irving Howe, "Lillian Hellman and the McCarthy Years," *Dissent*, 1976; collected in *Irving Howe: Selected Writings, 1950–1990* (New York: Harcourt Brace Jovanovich, 1990), 340–346.

18. Hellman, *Three*, 723.

19. Jackson R. Bryer, ed., *Conversations with Lillian Hellman* (Jackson: University Press of Mississippi, 1986), 212–13.

20. Hook, *Encounter*, February 1977.

21. Elia Kazan, *Elia Kazan: A Life* (New York: Knopf, 1988), 465.

22. www.pbs.org. American Masters.

23. Victor Navasky, *Naming Names* (New York: Viking, 1980), 243–44.

24. Benn Schulberg, *American Affairs*, February 2, 2011, http://suite101.com.

25. Bryer, ed., *Conversations with Lillian Hellman*, 249.

26. Hellman, *Scoundrel Time*, 114.

Chapter 13. Jewish Lit

1. Irving Howe, *World of Our Fathers* (New York: Harcourt, 1976), 585.

2. Sylvie Drake, in Jackson R. Bryer, ed., *Conversations with Lillian Hellman* (Jackson: University Press of Mississippi, 1986), 291.

3. Hellman, *Scoundrel Time*, 43.

4. Christine Doudna, in Bryer, *Conversations with Lillian Hellman*, 197.

5. Hellman, *Scoundrel Time*, 72.

6. Dashiell Hammett, *Selected Letters of Dashiell Hammett* (Washington, DC: Counterpoint, 2001), 611.

7. Francine Prose, *Anne Frank, The Book, The Life, The Afterlife* (New York: Harper, 2009), 177.

8. Prose, *Anne Frank*, 193.

9. Meyer Levin, *The Obsession* (New York: Simon and Schuster, 1973).

10. Prose, *Anne Frank*, 205.

11. Ralph Melnick, *The Stolen Legacy of Anne Frank: Meyer Levin, Lillian Hellman, and the Staging of the Diary* (New Haven: Yale University Press, 1997), 127, quoting Lewis Funke, *New York Times*, May 27, 1956.

12. Melnick, *Stolen Legacy*, 144, citing *New York Times*, May 8, 1956, Sunday News, May 13, 1956.

13. Cynthia Ozick, "Who Owns Anne Frank?" *The New Yorker*, October 6, 1997.

14. Hellman, *Three*, 439.

15. Tony Judt with Timothy Snyder, *Thinking the Twentieth Century* (New York: Penguin, 2012), 41.

16. Hellman, *Three*, 511.

17. Carl E. Rollyson, *Lillian Hellman: Her Legend and Her Legacy* (New York: St. Martin's Press, 1988), 413.

18. Lillian Hellman, *The Collected Plays* (Boston: Little, Brown, 1972), 767 (emphasis added).

19. Deborah Martinson, *Lillian Hellman: A Life with Foxes and Scoundrels* (Berkeley: Counterpoint Press, 2005), 292.

Chapter 14. An Honored Woman

1. Nora Ephron, *I Remember Nothing: And Other Reflections* (New York: Knopf, 2010), 87; Frances Kiernan, *Seeing Mary Plain: A Life of Mary McCarthy* (New York: W. W. Norton, 2000), 679.

2. Peter Adam, in Jackson R. Bryer, ed., *Conversations with Lillian Hellman* (Jackson: University Press of Mississippi, 1986), 229.

3. *New Republic*, January 1, 1966.

4. Hellman, *Three*, 206.

5. Lev Kopelev, *To Be Preserved Forever* (Philadelphia: J. B. Lippincott, 1977), Introduction by Lillian Hellman, 15.

6. R. D. Orlova, *Memoirs* (New York: Random House, 1983), 127–28.

7. Letter from Orlova quoted in Carl E. Rollyson, *Lillian Hellman: Her Legend and Her Legacy* (New York: St. Martin's Press, 1988), 432.

8. Hellman, *Three*, 182–3.

9. Hellman, *Three*, 186, 187.

10. Hellman, *Three*, 242.

11. William Wright, *Lillian Hellman: The Image, the Woman* (New York: Simon and Schuster, 1986), 311.

12. Marion Meade, *Dorothy Parker: What Fresh Hell Is This?* (New York: Villard, 1987), 413.

13. Wright, *Lillian Hellman*, interview with Teichmann, 311.

14. Bryer, ed., *Conversations with Lillian Hellman*, 136.

15. Hellman, *Three*, 266.

16. *Washington Post*, November 18, 1970.

17. Wright, *Lillian Hellman*, interview with Samuels, 339.

18. Alice Kessler-Harris, *A Difficult Woman: The Challenging Life and Times of Lillian Hellman* (New York: Bloomsbury, 2012), 66.

19. Wright, *Lillian Hellman*, 350.

20. Peter S. Feibleman, *Lilly: Reminiscences of Lillian Hellman* (New York: Morrow, 1988), 189.

21. Hellman, *Three*, 450–51.

22. Lillian Hellman, *Maybe* (Boston: Little, Brown, 1980), cover blurbs.

23. Rollyson, *Lillian Hellman*, 531, citing Water Clemons's review, *Newsweek*, June 2, 1980.

24. Hellman, *Maybe*, 43.

25. Feibleman, *Lilly*, 254.

26. Anatole Broyard, *New York Times*, May 13, 1980.

Chapter 15. Mere Facts

1. Alice Kessler-Harris, *A Difficult Woman: The Challenging Life and Times of Lillian Hellman* (New York: Bloomsbury, 2012), 203, citing notes for a Harvard lecture.

2. *New York Times*, August 23, 1969, Op-Ed piece attacking Soviet defector, Anatoly Kuznetsov.

3. Peter S. Feibleman, *Lilly: Reminiscences of Lillian Hellman* (New York: Morrow, 1988), 283.

4. Elizabeth Hardwick, Foreword to Mary McCarthy, *Intellectual Memoirs* (New York: Harcourt, 1992), x.

5. Mary McCarthy, "The Fact in Fiction," collected in *On the Contrary* (New York: Farrar, Straus, and Cudahy, 1961), 263.

6. *Paris Review*, Winter-Spring 1967.

7. Carol Brightman, *Writing Dangerously: Mary McCarthy and Her World* (New York: C. Potter, 1992), 603.

8. Frances Kiernan, *Seeing Mary Plain: A Life of Mary McCarthy* (New York: W. W. Norton, 2000), 670.

9. McCarthy, *Intellectual Memoirs*, 61.

10. Kiernan, *Seeing Mary Plain*, 671.

11. McCarthy, *On the Contrary*, 148.

12. Jackson R. Bryer, ed., *Conversations with Lillian Hellman* (Jackson: University Press of Mississippi, 1986), 61.

13. Carol Brightman, *Writing Dangerously*, 609.

14. *New York Times*, Charles Poore, May 18, 1957.

15. Mary McCarthy Papers, Vassar College Archives and Special Collections, Box 258, Material for Answering Interrogatory 15.

16. Mary McCarthy Papers, Box 258, Material for Answering First Interrogatory.

17. Rose Styron with Blakeslee Gilpin, eds., *Selected Letters of William Styron* (New York: Random House, 2012) 542–44, 556.

18. William Wright, *Lillian Hellman: The Image, the Woman* (New York: Simon and Schuster, 1986), 390.

19. Deborah Martinson, *Lillian Hellman: A Life with Foxes and Scoundrels* (Berkeley: Counterpoint Press, 2005), interview with Wexler, 355.

20. Rosalind Michahelles, quoted in Kiernan, *Seeing Mary Plain*, 681.

21. Martha Gellhorn, "Guerre de Plume," *Paris Review* No. 79, 1981.

22. Mary McCarthy to Ben O'Sullivan, August 17, 1980, quoted in Kiernan, *Seeing Mary Plain*, 681.

23. Norman Podhoretz, *Ex-Friends: Falling Out with Allen Ginsberg, Lionel and Diana Trilling, Lillian Hellman, Hannah Arendt, and Norman Mailer* (New York: Free Press, 1999), 122–23.

24. Feibleman, *Lilly*, 148.

25. Podhoretz, *Ex-Friends*, 123.

26. *The New Review*, May 1974.

27. Jackson R. Bryer, ed., *Conversations with Lillian Hellman* (Jackson: University Press of Mississippi, 1986), 195.

28. Edwin McDowell, *New York Times*, April 29, 1983.

29. Wright, *Lillian Hellman*, 408.

30. Joan Mellen, *Hellman and Hammett: The Legendary Passion of Lillian Hellman and Dashiell Hammett* (New York: HarperPerennial, 1997), 448–49, citing memo from Blair Clark.

31. Mary McCarthy deposition.

32. Prudence Crowther, ed., *Don't Tread on Me, The Selected Letters of S. J. Perelman* (New York: Viking, 1989), 288–89.

33. Carol Brightman, *Writing Dangerously*, 617.

34. "On the Frontier," *The New York Review of Books*, November 7, 2011.

ACKNOWLEDGMENTS

WHOEVER UNDERTAKES to write about Lillian Hellman owes a large debt to Hellman's previous biographers—to William Wright, Carl Rollyson, Deborah Martinson, Joan Mellen, and Alice Kessler-Harris—whose books I have read with great appreciation, and with pencil in hand. I am equally indebted to Diane Johnson and Richard Layman, for their work on Dashiell Hammett's life. Of course none of these authors bear responsibility for my interpretations, misinterpretations or conclusions.

Many thanks to my editor, Ileene Smith, who provoked and encouraged this book, and to my steadfast agent, George Borchardt. Dan Okrent listened to a writer's complaints and generously offered himself for much needed criticism at just the right moment. Victor Navasky disagreed with almost all my opinions about Lillian Hellman's politics, but graciously allowed that I had made a persuasive prosecutor's case. I am particularly grateful to Alan Goodman Koch, who unstintingly shared with me his years of research into Jewish life in nineteenth-century Demopolis, Alabama.

As if that was not enough, he and his wife, Linda, gave a stranger food and lodging, and provided her with a guided tour to the town and the residents of Hellman's family origins.

My husband, Ben Sonnenberg, my first reader for thirty years, died while I was working on this book. He remains as large as life to me. As always, I hope to make him proud.

INDEX

LH in index refers to Lillian Hellman. Works with no author indicated were written by Lillian Hellman.

JEWISH LIVES is a major series of interpretive
biography designed to illuminate the imprint of Jewish
figures upon literature, religion, philosophy, politics, cultural
and economic life, and the arts and sciences. Subjects are
paired with authors to elicit lively, deeply informed books that
explore the range and depth of Jewish experience
from antiquity through the present.

Jewish Lives is a partnership of Yale University Press
and the Leon D. Black Foundation.

Ileene Smith is editorial director. Anita Shapira and
Steven J. Zipperstein are series editors.